Grammar Without Groans

A Return to Standards in English

Ray and Chris Sparkes

PACKARD PUBLISHING LIMITED

CHICHESTER

Grammar Without Groans
A Return to Standards in English

© **Christopher James Sparkes, 2004.**
Reprinted with amendments, 2006.

The first edition of this book © the late James Raymond Sparkes, 1981.

Published by Packard Publishing Limited, Forum House, Stirling Road, Chichester, West Sussex, PO19 7DN.

ISBN-10: 1 85341 134 5
ISBN-13: 9 78185 341 134 2
(published in softback only)

A CIP catalogue record for this book is available from the British Library.

Designed by Louise Burston.
Typeset by Dorwyn Limited, Wells, Somerset.
Printed in the United Kingdom by DPS Partnership Limited, Burgess Hill, West Sussex.

Contents

PREFACE TO THE FIRST EDITION

The purpose of this book is to present the correct usages of the English language in an informal and entertaining way.

It is free of any of those formalities which impose such exercises as parsing and analysis on minds more attuned to the murmur of summer outside. As the reader will soon discover, it is not necessary to possess a knowledge of moods, cases, clauses and similar terminology to decide what is right or wrong with a sentence (such technical matters can be left for other contexts).

There is a note of sweet reason underlying all our codes of Standard English, and with the aid of this book readers should have little difficulty in applying that reason to all that is set before them. Moreover, they should also discover that to brush up their correct English usage is to indulge in a pleasant and fascinating diversion. For lively minds, simplified grammar need never be dull.

For the most part, the rules have been based on the principles of common usage and a knowledge of the true meaning of words. Such rules are simple to understand and easy to remember, particularly if readers will cheerfully test themselves on the many questions presented at the end of every chapter. There is also a general test section dealing with every aspect of standard usage that the book has covered. A complete list of answers appears at the end.

Finally, I would like to stress that, as the book's title suggests, this is an informal guide to correct English, and in no way is intended to contradict the more formal lessons of English grammar for those whose needs and inclinations demand them. I am convinced, nevertheless, that it is quite possible to speak and write correct and accurate English without first having to acquaint onself with the more rigid terminology of a formal textbook. I can only hope that the presentation of this little book will help to convince others too.

Ray Sparkes (*1981*)

PREFACE TO THE SECOND EDITION

The mechanics of writing are the subject of what we call *grammar*. It has been studied since classical times. Grammar is the set of rules used for forming units of words into meaningful sentences.

The correct use of language, punctuation and syntax (word order) so as to create meaning are the constituents of good grammar, not only in Standard English, but in any language, written or spoken. It is not just that bad grammar sounds uneducated. It is more serious than that. Bad grammar clouds your meaning, and leads to ambiguity, obscurity and, eventually, barbarism.

The best writers have to concern themselves with good grammar. On the other hand, those who are not careful with grammar cannot be good writers. Good grammar is a courtesy to your reader. It has nothing to do with accent, class or snobbery. It is equivalent to the architect's plans of a building's design. And good punctuation is equivalent to the pauses and timing of a skilful orator. They help you to say what you mean.

Twenty years after *Grammar Without Groans* was first published, it still impresses me. As a teacher of Linguistics and Creative Writing, I refer to it often, and make good use of it in my teaching. It has the benefit of explaining its points in a way that is accessible to students at any level. That is one of the reasons why I have wanted to make a new edition.

Readers familiar with the first edition will, it is hoped, be delighted with the new format. They will probably notice that I have changed the order of the chapters slightly, in order to press together the topics in the most logical way. There are some new sections in Chapter 10, some expanded explanations, revised examples, and other modifications and twitches throughout the book. I have added a detailed index for quick reference to topics, as, once it has been read, that is the most frequent way it will be used.

I have also included, by way of an afterword, an argument in favour of holding onto the concept of standards in English, that is, standards which are aesthetically pleasing and agreeable forms of language. My father's attention to standard forms is surely a best of beginnings towards rejuvenation.

My father was not so prescriptive (nor so proscriptive) as some English grammarians, befitting, I suppose, his generosity of spirit. He did, though, have a strong aversion to certain non-standard forms (such as 'like' as a meaningless interjection), because of particularly ugly occurrences he heard as a school teacher. I find myself less pre-scriptive still, but I have tried to remain loyal in spirit to him. For we were certainly of one accord in the belief that language, like anything else – artworks, buildings, documents, literatures, treasures – needs its gatekeepers and guardians.

So, after more than twenty years, I believe that *Grammar Without Groans* is a book that should not only continue to be in print, but also remains one that should be in a reachable place on everybody's desk.

Chris Sparkes (*2004*)

Note: an asterisk* placed after a word in the text denotes that it is an incorrect form.

Most people who bother with the matter at all would admit that the English language is in a bad way, but it is generally assumed that we cannot by conscious action do anything about it. Our civilization is decadent and our language – so the argument runs – must inevitably share in the general collapse. ... The point is that the process is reversible. Modern English, especially written English, is full of bad habits which spread by imitation and which can be avoided if one is willing to take the necessary trouble. If one gets rid of these habits one can think more clearly ... (George Orwell, *Inside the Whale*, Penguin, 1957, p. 143)

Chapter 1

BETWEEN YOU AND ME

BETWEEN 'YOU' AND 'ME'

Perhaps you are sometimes puzzled over the correct use of 'you' and 'me' and 'you' and 'I'. Some people, many of them educated, are often guilty of error when using them. For some reason, a number of people imagine it is more correct to say, 'Will you have coffee with Jane and I?' Would they be right? Grammatically they would be wrong. Can you say why? There is no need to worry any further if you are not sure, because there happens to be a simple rule that will prevent you from ever again making a mistake over the terms 'you' and 'me' and 'you' and 'I'.

Let us consider for a moment the sentence 'Will you have coffee with Jane and I?' Suppose Jane wasn't there. Suppose you had invited someone to have coffee with only you. Would you then say, 'Will you have coffee with I?' No, you would say, 'Will you have coffee with me?' Why then change 'me' to 'I' when Jane is included?

There is, therefore, a simple rule that will never let you down. Wherever you would say 'us', use 'you and me'; wherever you would say 'we', then say 'you and I'. Here are four examples:

If you and I (we) are correct in our judgement, we have at last found the man we are looking for.

I am not sure that this concert will appeal to you and me (us).

Do you remember the day you and I (we) decided to go to Florence?

I feel sure that Mr Crumbs will be delighted to talk things over with you and me (us).

TEST YOURSELF

Perhaps you would like to consider these six sentences. Two are wrong. Can you say which?

1. We will receive a bonus if you and I put in extra time.
2. I cannot understand why he should have mistaken you and me for two other people.
3. I cannot recall when such a happy event has happened to you and I.
4. The next time he asks David and me to play tennis, I hope he will have learned the rules.
5. It's all very well for you and I to rejoice over our good fortune, but what about those who were less lucky?
6. Perhaps you would share your umbrella with Tony and me?

Chapter 2

THE UNRELATED PARTICIPLE
or in other words
when brief-cases dash round corners, churches rush to the top of hills, windows climb ladders, fishes sit comfortably on bridges and finches focus field-glasses.

You have no need of the knowledge of grammatical terms in order to spot what is wrong with the sentences given below. The note of sweet reason alone will tell you why they make nonsense, and yet the extraordinary thing is that such mistakes occur every day. But once you have seen the ridiculous side of this kind of thing, you will not fall into making the same errors. Consider this example first of all:

Dashing round the bend, the brief-case fell in the mud.

As this sentence stands – and if it is to be taken literally – we are to assume that the brief-case dashed round the bend. There is nothing here to suggest that *I* or *you* or *he* or *she* were dashing round the bend; there is not a single mention of yourself, nor of anybody. So who, then, was going round the bend? We do not know. The only facts stated are those of dashing round the bend and a brief-case falling in the mud. Here are a few more examples:

Rushing to the top of the hill, the church lay in front of me.

Climbing to the top of the ladder, the window was in easy reach.

Sitting comfortably on the bridge, the fish soon began to bite.

Focusing the field-glasses on the tree, the finches came into sight.

Taking a careful aim with the rifle, the bottle was smashed to pieces.

If we read these literally we see that:

(a) a church rushed to the top of a hill,
(b) a window climbed a ladder,
(c) fish sat comfortably on a bridge,
(d) finches focused field-glasses,
(e) a bottle took careful aim.

Yes, we see what was really meant (although without the contexts we do not know who were performing the actions in the first parts of the sentences). But remaining as they are, these sentences, if we may term them as such, add up to nonsense. They are nonsense because there is no given link between the actions and their implied subjects. To correct them into good English we need to recast them entirely to include some persons who are performing the actions of the verbs, such as:

As we rushed to the top of the hill, we saw the church lying in front of us.

When I had climbed to the top of the ladder, I found the window lay within easy reach of my hand.

I seated myself in comfort on the bridge, cast my line, and the fish soon began to bite.

As I focused the field-glasses on the tree, the finches came into sight.

Taking careful aim with my rifle, I fired, and the shot smashed the bottle to pieces.

In every instance you will notice that the 'doer', or performer, of the action is mentioned. At the same time, the performer is not so far removed from the main stem of the action in which the ambiguity arises. You will probably realize also that opening sentences participles ending with 'ing' does not create good style, so it is better to avoid the habit for both grammatical and stylistic reasons.

If you will just recast some other 'sentences' that follow, I doubt that you will ever be guilty of making similar mistakes. There is, of course, more than one way of writing them correctly, and the answers in the Answer section are only suggestions in order to help you correct the mistakes.

TEST YOURSELF
1. Sitting on his horse, the sea lay below him.
2. Jumping over the fence, my knee was badly bruised.
3. An oak dressing-table is for sale, by a lady, newly-polished.
4. Before giving this medicine to the baby, shake it vigorously.
5. Painting all day, the picture gradually grew into something worth hanging.
6. Dancing all over the ballroom floor, Jane's head was in a whirl.
7. Cycling round the corner, the wheel fell off.

Chapter 3

RELATIVE PRONOUNS
such as
'who' and 'whom'

Confusion often occurs over the use of 'who' and 'whom'. These words are known as relative pronouns. The use of them depends on whether the person concerned performs the actions, or has the action performed on him or her. To make this clearer, let us consider two sentences, each of which contains either 'who' or 'whom'.

Jack Kendall is the man who ran a mile yesterday.

This is the man whom I interrupted.

In the first sentence, Jack is the person who performed the action. He ran a mile. He is the only person mentioned. He is the performer of the action – he ran a mile. We know that, apart from anything else, everyday usage is enough to convince us that 'who' is the correct word. Even so, it will be useful to keep in mind, especially when we come across less obvious sentences – that Jack Kendall performed the action.

In the second sentence, the only action performed (by the 'doer' of the verb) is by the narrator of the sentence, 'I' (known in grammar as the *first person singular*). I interrupted this man. The man whom I interrupted does nothing. He stands in isolation to the performer of the verb. It is the 'I' who does the interrupting. When, therefore, a person stands in isolation to the performer, then 'whom' is the correct word to use.

Consider again, for proof of this, the following four sentences:

This is the man who went past our house last night.

Michael Atherton was a batsman whom all opposition

bowlers respected.

It was Jim Fawcett, the secret service agent, whom they arrested.

We were approached by a policeman who politely asked us what we wanted.

These examples are, no doubt, clear enough, and would seem to give adequate proof of what we have been saying, that is, that the performer of the verb is 'who', and that the receiver of the performance is 'whom'. Nevertheless, there are other instances where this rule is not so apparent, and where an understanding of the meaning of the sentence must be the truest guide. Why, for instance, does the following sentence require 'whom'?

Uncle Henry, whom we were all expecting tomorrow, arrived today.

You may say that, since Uncle Henry performed the action – he arrived today – the correct word to use should be 'who'. But here it will be noticed, the clause 'whom we were all expecting tomorrow' has been put in a parenthetical sense, that is, within commas, and is incidental to the main stem (or clause) of the sentence which is 'Uncle Henry arrived today'. Within the parenthesis our rule still holds good; the verb 'were ... expecting' was performed by the 'we', not by Uncle Henry.

TEST YOURSELF
And now you might care to test yourself by inserting the correct word in the blank spaces below:

1. We arrived just in time to save the prisoners, many of —— had already given up hope.
2. It is difficult to say —— is responsible for this action.
3. Mr Blunder, by —— we were invariably amused, came to dinner last night.
4. Did I hear you say it was John —— rescued the climbers?

5. Jane, —— was not at all suspicious, walked into the room.
6. This is the man to —— I owe a debt of allegiance.

DISTINCTION BETWEEN WRITTEN AND SPOKEN ENGLISH

When we speak, we sometimes use 'who' instead of the strictly grammatically correct 'whom'. In the following example we should be speaking rather like an old-fashioned textbook if we said 'whom'. Suppose, for example, you were called to the telephone. You would no doubt say to the person who received the call, 'Who did you say it was?' The reply might well be, 'Guess – who do think it is?' You could use the grammatical 'whom' and bask in the knowledge of being very correct, but you would hardly be using every-day English. There is a distinction to be made between written and spoken English, and sometimes (though not always) the spoken version, even if not grammatically correct, is nevertheless accepted as normal colloquial usage.

FURTHER POINTS TO REMEMBER

Other relative pronouns (apart from 'who' and 'whom', which we have just seen) are 'whose', 'which' and 'that'. It is useful to remember the uses of these three words:

1. 'who', 'whom' and 'whose' refer to persons;
2. 'which' refers to animals and things;
3. 'that' refers to animals and things, and sometimes to persons.

Here are examples of the three words in use:

1. This is the man *who* betrayed his country.
   This is the man *whom* they caught red-handed.
   This is the man *whose* case is being reviewed.

2. This is the zebra *which* was injured.   (animal)
   This is the patio *which* I designed.   (thing)

3. This is the zebra *that* was injured.   (animal)

This is the patio *that* I designed. (thing)

This is the man *that* they caught red-handed. (person)

The words 'who' and 'that' are often used interchangeably (as relative pronouns) when used in relation to persons, though 'who' is always preferable. Not all relative pronouns, though, can be used for animals and things.

Chapter 4

'SHE' AND 'I' — 'HER' AND 'ME'

Is it 'them' – or 'they'
Or 'us' – or simply 'we'?
Let's look again – and see.

The rule applying to 'you and I' and 'you and me' (Chapter 1) applies just as validly to 'she and I' and 'her and me'. Where you can use 'we', you can also say 'she and I'. Where you can use 'us', you can also say 'her and me'. The truth of this rule can be seen from the following:

The decision to hold another meeting was left to her and me (us).

It is not often that she and I (we) are asked to play violins.

Mistakes often arise, however, over words such as 'them', 'they', 'us' and 'we'. Consider, for example, these two sentences:

We can cook better than they (them).

Jim is able to paint landscapes much better than we (or us?).

We can soon discover which are the correct words by extending the sentences a little further than the full-stop:

We can cook better than they (can cook).

Jim is able to paint better landscapes than we (can paint them).

We see now that 'they' and 'we' are the better pronouns to use.

But perhaps a safer rule to remember is that the performers of the action are 'I', 'she', 'they' or 'we'. Those at the receiving end of the action, or who do not perform any action at all, are 'me', 'her', 'them' and 'us'.

Let us look for a moment or two at some of these performers in action. Where it is possible, we will extend the sentence a little farther than the full-stop – a sign of additional proof:

It was I who gave the firemen the warning.

Few people can sprint as rapidly as he (can sprint).

Who opened the window? It was she (who opened the window).

Mr Perkins was anxious to prove that he could play the piano just as skilfully as they (could play the piano).

And now, let us turn our attention to some of the receivers of the action, or those who perform no action at all:

It was to her, and all her kind, that the speech was addressed.

Everyone had departed from the platform except him.

We thought it was very considerate of them to leave twenty pence for the 'phone call. (True, they left the twenty pence, but it was 'we' who did the thinking.)

It has been said of us that we are a nation of shopkeepers.

A further word or two, however, about the 'performers': although we have seen already how they take on the complements of 'I', 'he', 'she', 'they', or 'we', it is nevertheless fair to warn readers about too much pedantry. For example, in response to the question 'Who is it?' the answer, strictly speaking, should be 'It is I', but few people, I imagine, would reply as pedantically as that. Colloquially, we say, 'It's me', just as the French would reply 'C'est moi'. Use 'it is I' in writing if you like, but I suppose it is a matter of temperament whether you care to use it in everyday speech. As long as you know what you are doing, the onus is really on you.

TEST YOURSELF

Six of the following eight sentences are wrong:

1. She suffers much more from chilblains than me.
2. You are a much fairer girl than her.
3. It is obvious that the washing-up is going to be left to her and me.
4. I was surprised to learn that him and me had been asked to play.
5. I was reluctant to admit that Tim could walk for a longer period than I.
6. The prize was to be shared between him and I.
7. Do you think you could toss the pancakes as high as her?
8. Everyone present, except she, was asked to sing at the party.

Before we close the chapter, perhaps we should consider four sentences. It may not be easy at first glance to decide whether they are right or wrong.

Jane loves you more than I.

Jane loves you more than me.

Grandfather is more suspicious of you than I.

Grandfather is more suspicious of you than me.

Which sentences are correct? The truth is they can all be correct. It depends on what we mean. If we mean in the first example that Jane loves you more than I love you, and, second, we mean that Jane loves you more than she loves me, then both sentences are correct. If the same test is applied to the third and fourth examples, then they, of course, are also right.

You may, incidentally, care to cast a similar line of thought on 'Test Yourself' question 1 (above). Do we really mean that she suffers much more from chilblains than she suffers from me?

Chapter 5

TAKING POSSESSION

'Him' or 'his'? – 'You' or 'your'? – 'Me' or 'my'?
'Us' or 'our'? – 'Them' or 'their'?

Errors often occur when words such as 'him', 'you', 'me', 'us', and 'them' are used instead of 'his', 'your', 'my', 'our', and 'their'. This will become all the more clear if we take three examples and see where they go wrong:

I object to him staying out late.

She showed no surprise at you arriving late.

Martha was rather frightened at me banging the door.

In the first sentence, was it really to 'him' that I objected? I objected, surely, to what he did. It was his action that incurred my displeasure; to him personally I may have had no objection at all. To put the sentence right, we must put the 'him' into 'his' because it is his action to which I object. So the correct sentence is:

I object to his staying out late.

As we have dealt with the first error, so similarly do we deal with the second. No doubt the error is apparent already. Did she really show no surprise at 'you'? No, she showed no surprise at 'your' action, your action of arriving late.

Third, was Martha rather frightened at 'me'? Not at all: she was rather frightened by what I did, 'my' banging the door.

Should you find yourself still in difficulty over these sentences – if, for instance, you are not sure whether to turn 'me' into 'my', or 'you' into 'your' and so on – there is a simple test which you can quickly apply to errors of this kind. Imagine that a sentence is suddenly broken in half, like this:

I will have to think carefully about you/deciding to go to Paris.

The first half of the sentence implies that I shall have to think carefully about 'you'. But is this what is intended? Not at all; it was about what you did – 'your' action of deciding to go to Paris. Turn 'you' into 'your' and the sentence is correct:

I will have to think carefully about your deciding to go to Paris.

TEST YOURSELF

See if you can spot what is either right or wrong in the following seven sentences. Five are wrong.

1. The farmer did not mind them going into his orchard.
2. Mary said that she was not surprised at your going away.
3. I have not the slightest objection to you playing cricket on the lawn.
4. I remember him asking me if I had been to Milan to watch the football.
5. She was not amused at my bringing mud into the kitchen.
6. We were all surprised at you standing for Parliament.
7. I hope you have not been inconvenienced by us arriving late.

FURTHER POINTS TO REMEMBER

If, in the seven sentences above, the person or persons had been referred to by name, instead of 'you', 'me', 'us' and so on, and if, for instance, it had been John who played cricket on the lawn, or Mr Smith who had caused us all surprise by standing for Parliament, then the name would have been followed by an apostrophe 's'. (See Chapter 12 for further guidance on apostrophes.) For example, 'I have not the slightest objection to John's playing cricket on the lawn'; and 'We were all surprised by Mr Smith's standing for Parliament.' Our old friend, the 'possessive' again. Applying the same test as before, we can easily prove if the name requires a possessive 's':

I have not the slightest objection to John/playing cricket on the lawn.

Again, I did not mean that I haven't the slightest objection to John; I mean I have no objection to what he does, or is about to do. We see therefore that John does require a possessive sign, and we correct the error by saying,

I have not the slightest objection to John's playing cricket on the lawn.

So we can also say – this time quite rightly – that:

We were surprised at Bill's staying out so late.

I could not understand my uncle's objecting to my simple request.

To sum up: when the pronouns 'him', 'you', 'us' and 'them' – as well as proper nouns, first names, surnames and so on – are placed immediately before such verbal nouns as 'staying' or 'objecting' – as in the examples we have seen – then they invariably take the possessive form.

As always, of course, it will be the meaning and the sense of the sentence that will be your guide. Just to quote, what seems at first sight to be the reverse of all the foregoing, we see in the sentence:

John, slamming the door behind him, surprised us all.

This time we really are surprised by John himself. But a second glance tells us immediately that the commas have separated John from what he did. The sense of it all tells what is meant, and it tells us too that in this instance there is no question of John's possessing anything. A little sweet reason is always our truest guide.

'THEM' AND 'THOSE'

Finally, beware of the commonly spoken slang, 'Throw us *them* post-bags, will you?' (Or, even worse, 'Throw us *them those* post-bags, will you?') The correct, simple and attractive version of course is 'Throw us *those* post-bags...'.

These two words, 'them' and 'those' have different purposes, so that they are not interchangeable. 'Them' is a personal pronoun, used for the object of a sentence: 'I like *them*', whereas 'those' is called a demonstrative pronoun, used for pointing: 'I like *those* boots'. For some reason, the use of 'them' for 'those' has become widespread among uneducated speakers, but it should be avoided.

Chapter 6

HOW TO BE LOYAL TO YOUR SUBJECTS
The Government is, or the Government are?

When we think, speak and write in English, we fall naturally into the way of making our verbs and pronouns agree with the subject of the sentence. When we make our verbs and pronouns correspond, it depends on whether the subject is plural or singular. Nevertheless, there are many sentences which give rise to confusion, and this is because we use some words so often that we tend to overlook their real meaning. But before we look at some examples, perhaps a word or two about the subject of a sentence might not be amiss.

'ANYBODY', 'EVERYBODY', 'NOBODY'
These three words are pronouns.

Some textbooks (though, in fairness, not all) will sometimes tell you that the subject of a sentence is 'what the sentence is about' – which is about the vaguest way possible of defining what a subject really is. If we read the sentence 'The white horse galloped over the hills', then the sentence is not only about the white horse but is also about his galloping over the hills. In other words, we are no more knowledgeable about what is the subject than we were before. That vague textbook definition, then, is not too helpful. No, the real test of the subject is this: who, or what, performed the verb? In the sentence quoted, the white horse performed the verb – he did the galloping. Now, if we bear in mind that the verbs and pronouns must agree in number with the subject of a sentence, then we are not likely to fall into serious error. And yet, as I say, one or two words cause confusion. Consider, for instance, the sentence:

Everybody has given me their word they will be here by seven.

You will notice that 'everybody', being singular, has been followed by the singular verb 'has' (and not the plural form 'have'). But the sentence, oddly enough, goes on to refer to the plural forms 'they' and 'their'.

Perhaps the difficulty arises even more in spoken English. Take, for example, the following sentence spoken by a chairman:

I would like everybody who is in agreement with the motion to show their hands.

The chairman should have finished his sentence with 'his hand'. His mistake occurred for two reasons: first, because the plural words 'their' and 'hands' have not corresponded with their singular subject everybody' and the singular verb 'is'; second, because the word 'everybody' has been mistaken for the word 'all'. 'Everybody' is a collective noun which means 'every single person'. If you should doubt this, then ask yourself why the sentence begins with the singular verb 'has', that is, 'Everybody *has*...'. We would never find ourselves saying, 'Everybody *have*...'.

But what if the chairman had been addressing a mixed audience? Certainly he would have been grammatically correct by saying, 'I would like everybody who is in agreement with the motion to show his or her hand', but the sentence then becomes long, awkward and inelegant. It is better, for the sake of euphony (pleasantness of sound) to recast the sentence and replace 'everybody' by 'all', and so retain '*their* hands' as the natural complement. The chairman would have been better saying:

I would like all in agreement to raise their right hands.

Other words in this category are 'anybody' and 'nobody': 'If anybody has...'; 'Nobody has...'. The literal meanings of those are, 'If any person has...' and 'Not a single person has', so the pronouns take singular verbs.

COLLECTIVE NOUNS

Collective nouns are frequently used in a way which is, strictly speaking, incorrect. One often hears over the radio the technically incorrect 'The Government *are* meeting today about the fuel crisis', or 'Scotland *are* playing Ireland at Murrayfield on Saturday'. What is meant is 'The members of the Government are meeting today...' or 'The Scotland rugby team members are playing...' It is more colloquial to say 'The Government *are*...' and 'Scotland *are*...' But colloquial usage has shortened such lengthy and rather awkward sentences and left the plural 'are' related to a singular subject. It is, though, just as quick – and more logical – to use 'is' in such cases. So:

The Government is meeting today to discuss the fuel crisis.

There are circumstances, though, when it would be awkward to persist with pure grammatical correctness merely for the sake of it. In a race, say, two or three Kenyan runners may be among the race leaders. We would be more likely to say, 'Kenya *are* pressing ahead,' or, 'Kenya *are* dominating this race'. It would sound strange if we were to say, 'Kenya *is* pressing ahead', even if it is, strictly speaking, correct.

'NONE', 'NEITHER' AND 'EITHER'

There are, of course, other words which over time tend to lose their original meanings – words that are often mistaken for plural subjects when they ought to be singular. Words in this category are 'each', 'none', 'either' and 'neither'.

A tip that will help you with the use of 'none' is to think of its true meaning of 'not one'. It would be clumsy to say 'not one are...', so you know that 'none' is always followed by a singular verb. Remember, too, that the word 'neither' is usually followed by 'nor'. 'Either' – when the sense of the sentence demands it – is followed by 'or', as in the line, 'Either Tom or Dick is going to the zoo'.

TEST YOURSELF

Here are five sentences, each one of which is wrong. Can you say how they ought to have been written? The answers are at the end of the book.

1. Neither of these two parcels are light enough for Jane to carry.
2. I want each man in this room to place their votes in the box.
3. None of the cricketers I have mentioned have yet scored over fifty.
4. Neither John nor Henry have accepted the Robinsons' invitation.
5. Anybody who has recently voted for the Mayor's suggestion should reconsider their decisions.

ANOTHER WORD OR TWO ABOUT LOYALTY TO SUBJECTS

There are times when many things or persons are mentioned and yet are still followed by a singular verb. For example:

The captain, as well as his crew and the hundred and forty passengers, was saved.

The singular verb 'was' is used because it is being loyal to its subject 'captain'. Although others are mentioned – the crew and passengers – they are added as a parenthetical thought, and they are subordinate to the main subject. It is only when other things or persons are joined to the main subject that the verb becomes plural, as in, 'The captain, his crew and the passengers were saved'.

Other examples of this singular verb can be seen from the following:

The Queen, accompanied by the Duke, was present at the ceremony.

A knowledge of ornithology, together with various other aspects of nature lore, is necessary for the true enjoyment of country life.

The electrician, aided by his mate, is going to install some new wiring.

The novel *Under the Greenwood Tree*, to say nothing of other books on fishing, cricket and the poems of Robert Frost, was by his bedside.

TEST YOURSELF

As a helpful exercise, reconstruct each of those sentences so that it becomes correct to turn the singular verb into the plural. You will have to omit certain words and replace them by others, for example, 'The Queen and the Duke were present at the ceremony'.

Chapter 7
'MORE' AND 'MOST'

Mark Antony in *Julius Caesar* makes the remark, 'This was the most unkindest cut of all'. It would be unfair, however, to accuse Shakespeare of being ungrammatical. Elizabethan English was different from our own. The fault does not lie with Shakespeare; it is simply that language in common use, like coinage, undergoes changes and new customs. (There were, for instance, various ways of spelling Shakespeare's name.) And it is probable that Shakespeare included the extra syllable in order to comply with the ten-syllable pentameter in which he wrote his blank verse.

Nevertheless, if we were to compare Mark Antony's remark with modern English usage, we should have to admit that 'most unkindest' is grammatically wrong. Antony – again to judge by modern standards – was in fact breaking the rule of the comparative and the superlative. It will help us to make this rule clearer if we look at the following table:

Descriptive	Comparative	Superlative
tall	taller	tallest
heavy	heavier	heaviest
beautiful	more beautiful	most beautiful
wonderful	more wonderful	most wonderful

The words 'more' and 'most' are sometimes known as adverbs, but they are more properly defined as intensifiers, because they intensify the effects of adjectives and adverbs. (They are also sometimes known as 'comparators'.)

When we are comparing two things, two parcels for example, we say that one is heavier than the other. Notice, we say one is heavier when there are two. When there are more than two parcels, we then say that one of them, among all the others, is the heaviest.

We do not put the intensifiers 'more' or 'most' before words ending in the suffixes 'er' or 'est', such as 'more taller', 'more tallest', or, indeed, 'most unkindest' (unless quoting Shakespeare). Why should we? After all, if a girl happens to be the tallest in the room, then she is the tallest – she does not require the additional qualification of 'most'. You may say, of course, that she is the 'most tall' or, if you are comparing only two girls, that one is 'more tall' ('taller') than the other, but it is an offence against the sophistication and purity of English usage to say 'more taller' or 'most tallest'. Similarly we can say that one parcel is 'more heavy' (or 'heavier') than another one, or that a parcel is the 'most heavy' ('heaviest') among several others. So we should never use 'more heavier' or 'most heaviest'.

We also place the intensifiers 'more' and 'most' before those adjectives of three syllables or more, such as beautiful, wonderful, graceful or bountiful – long words that do not take on the endings of 'er' and 'est'. We say of two things that one is 'more beautiful' than another one, or that such and such a painting is the 'most beautiful' of all.

TEST YOURSELF

See if you have understood the principles in this chapter by spotting the errors in the following seven sentences. Three are right, four are wrong:

1. This girl is the most pretty of the two.
2. I think the painting by Constable is more beautiful than the one by Turner.
3. That statue over there is the most ugliest I have ever seen.
4. Of the two women Mrs Polly looks the most sadder.
5. Sarah is more graceful than Jane by far.
6. Of the five bowlers in the England side, Gough seems the more accurate.
7. Five men worked at the roadside, and of these the smallest man proved to be the most capable.

Chapter 8

'LIE' AND 'LAY' — 'LYING' AND 'LAYING'
or when grandfather lays eggs

'I'm afraid my grandfather is laying down,' said the small boy who opened the door.

What exactly was he laying? The carpet? Eggs?

The habit of confusing 'lying' with 'laying' is extraordinarily widespread, even among those whose grammar is otherwise reasonably good. The mistake occurs because the practitioners of the error have never really stopped to ask themselves what the words 'lying' and 'laying' really mean.

People even tell their dogs to lay down. Lay down what? Not bricks or concrete slabs surely.

These asides, flippant though they may be, should help us to remember more clearly what those words mean.

Perhaps the confusion has arisen because, although the word 'lay' can have other meanings, in the past tense it is 'lay' (I am going to 'lie' down; I 'lay' down yesterday). The word 'lay' actually has nothing whatever to do with stretching oneself in a reclining position. Let us see if we can remove the confusion by looking at the following explanation:

Lying means reclining, a restful posture. It also means telling lies.

Laying means the act of depositing something, putting something down. So, a man may be in the act of laying a carpet or laying down the law, a woman laying the table before a meal, or a bird producing an egg.

We see, therefore, that it is impossible for a dog to 'lay down', unless, of course, it might be 'laying' down some object such as its bone. But in ninety-nine cases out of a hundred, we know that dog-owners do not mean that, just as the small boy who opened the door and said that his grandfather was laying down did not mean that his grandfather had gone upstairs to lay down carpet or linoleum.

And now to 'lie' and 'lay':

Lie means both to _recline_ and _to tell a lie_.

Lay means _to deposit, put something down_. But it can also mean the past tense of 'lie'.

So we see that the verb 'to lie' does not take any object: this is known as an intransitive verb. We don't lie anything down: we just lie down. By contrast, 'to lay' always takes an object: this is known as a transitive verb. We don't just lay down: we lay something down. Before we begin to test ourselves by way of several examples, a few words remain to be said about 'laid' and 'lain':

Lain is what is called the past participle of 'lie' and has nothing whatever to do with laying anything down. It is preceded by the various forms of the verb 'have', that is, 'has', 'had', 'having', and can nearly always be substituted for 'been lying'.

Laid is the past tense of 'lay' – to put something down – for example, 'The gardener laid a path across the rose-bed'.

Examples of these in usage would be:

The cyclist had lain (been lying) in the ditch for two hours.

This tramp has lain (been lying) in the barn all night.

Perhaps this variety of verb forms is best presented for memory in a table:

Finite form	Participle form	Past tense participles
to tell lies, to be false:	lie (She is) lying	(She) lied, (She has) lied
to lie down, to recline:	lie down (She is) lying	(She has) lain
to put something down, or to produce eggs:	lay (She is) laying	(She) laid, (She has) laid

TEST YOURSELF

Fill in the correct words in the following eight sentences:

1. We had —— by the water's edge all the afternoon.
2. Mary was —— down the carpet when the guests arrived.
3. The old gentleman frequently went to —— down in the afternoons.
4. Few things are more delightful than to —— here under the willows.
5. The workmen —— the cable yesterday morning.
6. Trotty, our labrador, was —— on the couch when the vicar called.
7. 'The time has come,' said the gambler, to —— our cards on the table.
8. 'I have —— in wait for you,' said the stranger as he emerged from the shadows.

Chapter 9
OTHER COMMON ERRORS EXPLAINED

'A' OR 'AN'?

The words 'a' or 'an' standing before the name of something tells us that only 'one thing' is being described or spoken about. Examples are 'a book', 'a cat', 'a house', 'an apple', 'an onion', 'a uniform'. People are often confused about when to use the articles 'a' or 'an'.

The letter 'a', together with 'e', 'i', 'o' and 'u', is a vowel. All other letters of the alphabet are called consonants. We use 'a' before consonants: 'a book', 'a cat', 'a house' – and 'an' before vowels – 'an apple', 'an onion' and so on.

There are some words, however, whose first letters are not the ones sounded, for example, 'honest, 'heir', 'honour', 'hour', when we say 'onest', 'eir' (pronounced 'air'), 'onour', 'our'. These words start with vowel sounds and are used with 'an'.

We can see from the example of 'a uniform' that there is an exception for some words beginning with a vowel which also have consonant-sounding 'y' first letters: 'uniform' (yew-niform), 'unique' (yew-nique), 'unit' (yew-nit), 'union' (yew-nion), 'united' (yew-nited). They all require 'a' before them. 'An' precedes words that begin with proper 'u' sounds, for example, 'untidy' or 'underground'.

'AND' OR 'BUT'?

'And' and 'but' are conjunctions, linking words, which have slightly different uses. The word 'and' links both words (in lists) and clauses. Examples are:

Apples, pears, bananas and grapes are fruits.

I like coffee, and I like tea.

The word 'but' usually links clauses, phrases and words (not lists). And 'but' also introduces a degree of difference (known as 'adversative')

Bob plays cricket, but does not play football.

You may come, but please arrive early.

The first two examples show the simple linking of clauses. In the two examples using 'but', two clauses are linked, but the second parts seem to disagree with the first, or are different from them. They introduce a degree of difference. 'But' also links phrases and occasionally single words, as in 'Elaine likes all sports but boxing'.

ANY OTHER

It is sometimes said, for example, that the Bible has 'a larger circulation than any book'. If the Bible has a larger circulation than 'any book', then the Bible itself is included in the comparison. In other words, could the Bible have a larger circulation than its own? We mean, of course, that the Bible has a larger circulation than *any other* book. In comparisons of this kind, do not forget to include 'other'. For example:

Canaletto painted more pictures of Venice than any other painter.

'BETWEEN' AND 'AMONG'

'Between' is used when we refer to two things or persons, that is, 'These chocolates are to be shared *between* Bill and Harry'. 'Among' is used when we refer to more than two, that is, 'Will you please share these gifts *among* the people'.

'CAN' AND 'MAY'

These words are known as modal verbs, because they describe moods of potential and possibility, and they give description to other verbs: 'You can revise'; 'you may leave'. They are often misused, but there is no difficulty if we remember that 'can' means 'am I able to?' or 'is it possible?'. For example, 'I'll come if I can' (if the bus is running). The word 'may' implies permission or 'am I allowed to?' 'I'll come if I may' (if you will allow me). 'May' also expresses a wish or possibility (as does 'might'). Here are examples, some with replies that show the correct use:

'Can I catch the 39 bus here?'
'Yes, this is the right stop.'

'May I catch the 39 bus?'
'No. Finish your homework first.'

'Can I get a through ticket to Manchester?'
'Yes, of course.'
'May I have a Day Return then?'

'May success follow you always.'

'There may be no trains running.'

'CENTRE ON', 'REVOLVE AROUND'

One so often hears on radio or television and reads in newspapers sentences such as, 'The football club's publicity centred round the arrival of its new star striker', or, 'The economic difficulties of the country centred round its lack of natural resources'. The centre of a circle – from which the expression has been derived – is a unique point. Things can be centred *on* that point (sit on that spot), or they can revolve *around* it – but they cannot centre *around* it. It is better to write 'centre on' and 'revolve around'. So:

The football club's publicity centred on the arrival of its new star striker.

Most computer software development is centred on Silicon Valley, California.

and,

The economic difficulties of the country revolved around its lack of natural resources.

The success of the Springboks revolves around the scrummaging power of their forwards.

'DIFFERENT FROM'[1]

Perhaps because of the influence of American English, there has become a widespread habit of attaching to the word 'different' the preposition 'to'. You might hear people saying, 'My uniform is different *to* yours'. According to purists of standard usage, that would be considered incorrect and awkward. (They might also add that it is the word 'indifferent' which takes the preposition 'to' – a quite different word from [or, to] 'different'!).

Others, though, might consider it a richness in English that we have the availability of both prepositions, and, moreover, that it does not matter which is used.

Preference can only end as a matter of personal choice. Unlike other matters of grammar discussed in this book, the personal preference does not in any way affect meaning. For purists, though, they are not backed up by a Latin model, if, in any case, such a model has any value.

We should make the comment that in modes of formal writing, we would probably want to pay attention to formal correctness, whereas we would likely be less strict in speaking.

While on this subject, it is of interest that American English also uses the construction 'different *than*'. Although this may sound strange to English ears, it could very occasionally be useful, such as in, say, 'My musical tastes are different *than* last year', or, 'My ideas now are different *than* when I was young'. The usefulness of this is that it avoids the need of having to add into the sentence another clumsy (and pedantic) clause such as 'those which I held when...', which we would have to do if we began by saying that 'My ideas now are different *from*...', or 'My ideas now are different *to*...'.

---

[1] A prohibition on 'different *to*', and a corresponding insistence on 'different *from*', were described by the linguist Professor Jean Aitchison as 'a misguided attempt to make English behave more like Latin' (*Reith Lecture*, 1996). Her argument would have been stronger if she had said that the Latin verb for 'to differ' (*differo*) could take 'from', 'to' or 'with'.

'EACH' AND 'BOTH'; 'EACH OTHER' AND 'ONE ANOTHER'

'Each' means 'separately'. 'Both' means 'together'. It would be wrong to say, 'Both soldiers carried a rifle'. The reason is that it could denote that there was only one rifle, and it was being carried by two soldiers. If we said, 'Both soldiers carried rifles', this could denote any number of rifles. It is, therefore, more helpful to say, 'Each soldier carried a rifle' – so long as we recognize that 'each' denotes two soldiers.

'Each other' (occasionally written as a single word, 'eachother') is used when referring to two persons, 'one another' when referring to more than two. So,

The two friends immediately responded to each other.

and,

They all appeared to be fighting one another.

'IF I WERE'...

Use 'if I were' when the mood expresses some indefinable future possibility or hypothesis, such as, for example, 'If you were the only girl in the world and I were the only boy', or 'If I were a rich man, I would lay presents at your feet'.

'Was' is used when events have actually taken place. Why, for example, would it be wrong to use 'were' in the following?

If he was a hard boss, he was capable of some kindly and generous actions.

'Was' is correct here because that state of affairs had actually existed. In the past, indeed, he was a hard boss. But if we wish to imply some indefinite condition in the future, the state of which we have not yet experienced, it would be correct to say, 'If he were a hard boss, then I should not dream of working for him'. 'If I were' is used for the unlikely or improbable event.

'LESS' AND 'FEWER'

'Less' is used in reference to quantity, 'fewer' in reference to numbers. It is incorrect to say, 'There are *less** teachers in your college'. We should say, instead, 'There are *fewer* teachers in your college'. But when we refer to quantity, we naturally use 'less', as in 'There is *less* petrol in the tank than I thought' (but *'fewer* litres').

So, to cite some examples: *'fewer* footballs', *'less* courage', *'fewer* goals', *'less* training', *'fewer* cars', *'less* traffic'. Notice that the nouns following the word 'less' do not end with the letter s, whereas the words following 'fewer' all end with the letter s. This then gives us one rule for guidance.

The linguistic reason for the uses of 'fewer' and 'less' is that nouns in English are divided into two categories, *count* nouns and *non-count* nouns. The word 'petrol' is a non-count noun because, obviously, you cannot sit down and count petrol – so you would not talk about 'two or three petrols'*; therefore we say *'less* petrol'. (Just for the sake of argument, yes, we might possibly speak of 'three or four grades of petrol', which, hypothetically, we might shorten and say 'three or four petrols'). The word 'litres', though, is a count noun because it is a measurement in numbers; therefore we say *'fewer* litres'.

There is another rule for guidance as well. The words 'many' and 'fewer' belong to *count* nouns. So, for *count* nouns, you would either say 'many cars' or 'fewer cars'. On the other hand, the words 'much' and 'less' belong to *non-count* nouns. So, for *non-count* nouns, you would either say 'much milk' or 'less milk'. Further examples for *count* nouns are: *'many* goals', *'fewer* goals'; *'many* birds', *'fewer* birds'; *'many* children', *'fewer* children'. And further examples for *non-count* nouns are: *'much* courage', *'less* courage'; *'much* patience', *'less* patience'; *'much* petrol', *'less* petrol'. Conversely, we would not say *'much** goals', *'much** cars', *'much** children'.

These words 'fewer', 'less', 'many' and 'much' are known as determiners, because they determine number and quantity.

'LIKE' AND 'AS'

'Like' is used when two things are compared, such as 'My new coat is *like* yours', or again, 'Your painting is very *like* the one I saw in the exhibition'. The word 'like', however, should not be used as a joining word to anyone, or anything, performing an action.

Strictly speaking, it would not be correct to say, 'I am going to fasten up my coat *like* you do', or, 'John bowls a leg-break just *like* you bowl', or, 'It was *like* you said'. In formal writing these would sound sloppy. However, we must admit that in speech it might for some sound pedantic to use 'as' in these examples. It certainly would be pedantic – and probably offensive – to attempt to correct anybody for using 'like'. In each of the foregoing examples, the word 'like' should be exchanged for 'as'. So, 'Sheila is going to do her hair *as* Joan does hers'.

NEGATIVES, 'NEITHER' ... 'NOR', AND DOUBLE NEGATIVES

Some words express 'yes' (positive or affirmative), while others express 'no' (negative). Words such as 'either' have a positive meaning, while 'neither' is negative. Others in these categories of expressing 'yes' or 'no' are 'some' or 'all', as opposed to 'none', 'many' as opposed to 'few', 'ever' or 'always' as opposed to 'never'. Some positive pairs, and some negative pairs, work together:

You may have *either* egg mayonnaise or salami sandwiches for tea. (positive)

***Either* you *or* your sister will go night-clubbing. (positive)**

I have *neither* time *nor* money for a holiday. (negative)

***Neither* you *nor* I understands the problem. (negative)**

It is worth remembering that a double negative always makes an affirmative. In the sentence 'I should not be surprised if we don't have rain', I am really saying that I shall not be surprised if it keeps fine! But if I am expecting rain, I should of course have said that 'I shall not be surprised if we *do* have rain'. Sometimes we hear the following (slang) constructions spoken:

I've not had no dinner today.

I ain't had no dinner.

I don't want nothing.

The first really means 'I have had some dinner today'. The speaker, we presume, means to say, 'I've had no dinner today', or, 'I've not had any dinner today'. The second of course means 'I don't want anything', or, 'I want nothing'.

Other commonly heard clumsy (and very unattractive) slang expressions that should be avoided are:

I didn't used to like tomatoes. (Wrong)

I used not to like tomatoes. (Correct version)

I didn't ought to have done it. (Wrong)

I ought not to have done it. (Correct version)

OMITTING ESSENTIAL WORDS

The following sentence is wrong, but can you tell at a glance why?

Timothy's presence at the opera did not add but rather detracted from my enjoyment of the music.

If you cannot quite see why there is something not right about it, then let us omit the phrase 'but rather detracted from'. We are now left with 'Timothy's presence at the opera did not add – my enjoyment of the music'. We now see immediately that the preposition 'to' has been omitted. The sentence should of course read,

Timothy's presence at the opera did not add to, but rather detracted from, my enjoyment of the music.

An understanding of this kind of mistake will immediately give a clue to the errors in the following:

People who have devoted themselves to the study of nature, never have and never will lose their sense of wonder.

The fencer was as quick and perhaps quicker than his opponent.

In the first sentence, the writer has omitted the word 'lost'. It should have read:

People who have devoted themselves to the study of nature, never have lost and never will lose their sense of wonder.

In the second sentence, you will see that the writer should have inserted the word 'as' after 'quick'. It should therefore read,

The fencer was as quick as and perhaps quicker than his opponent.

'ONE OF THE BEST WHO HAVE...'

'Mark Waugh was undoubtedly one of the most stylish batsmen who have ever played for Australia.' This sentence is correct, but it is not uncommon to see the word (auxiliary verb) 'have' changed to 'has'. The folly of this can be seen if we reverse the order of the sentence, that is, to this: 'Of the most stylish batsmen who *has* (eh?) ever played for Australia...'. That should of course read as, 'Of the most stylish batsmen who *have* ever played for Australia...'. Mark Waugh is of course being compared to all the other batsmen who *have* played.

'ONLY'

This useful word (both adverb and adjective) is often misused or mis-placed in a sentence, thereby altering the meaning from the one intended. 'Only' says in effect, this thing, but not that one: this person, not someone else: that action, but no other: that place or time, rather than some other. It makes clear what we want to say and our meaning more exact, but we have to think carefully where the word is to be placed in a sentence:

1. **He only died a week ago. (Wrong – the sentence implies that that is all he did; but, though, he could**

have done something else instead.)
He died *only* a week ago. (Correct version)

2. *Only* the visiting preacher will preach at evening worship at St John's next Sunday. (Not St John's own preacher.)

3. The *only* visiting preacher will preach at evening worship at St John's next Sunday. (No other preacher is visiting.)

4. The visiting preacher will *only* preach at evening worship at St John's next Sunday. (He won't conduct the rest of the service.)

5. The visiting preacher will preach *only* at evening worship at St John's next Sunday. (He won't preach at morning worship as well.)

6. The visiting preacher will preach in the evening worship *only* at St John's next Sunday. (But not at another church down the road.)

7. The visiting preacher will preach at evening worship at St John's *only* next Sunday. (Not on any other Sunday.)

It is worth noting that the word 'only' is placed close to and before the word to be affected – unless perhaps for more emphasis, as in the last example, when we could say, 'The visiting preacher will preach at evening worship at St John's next Sunday only'.

'SCARCELY (OR HARDLY)...THAN'

'Scarcely...than' (or 'hardly...than') is a common error. The word 'than' should be replaced by 'when', denoting some incident of time. For example, 'Scarcely had I sat down to supper *when* the telephone rang', or again, 'I had hardly completed my first novel *when* the inspiration came to write another'.

'SHOULD' AND 'WOULD'; 'SHALL' AND 'WILL'

The hidden meanings (nuances) underlying 'should', 'would', 'shall' and 'will' are so confusing that even Fowler, compiler of the standard work, *Modern English Usage*, suggested that any definite explanation would perplex people even more. The four words are known as modal verbs, because they express moods of obligation, condition, and the future tense.

The use of 'I should' or 'I would' appears to come naturally to southern Englishmen, whereas it is customary for northerners to use the terms the other way round. It is sufficient, perhaps, to say that in most instances 'should' appears to carry with it some sense of obligation, as in, 'After thinking about it I feel I should go with you'. 'Would' carries a sense of probability, as in, 'If I had the funds, I would return to Italy'.

There is the story of an old Scot who was drowning, and despite his pleas the English onlookers did not move to save him. What, after all, were the purest speaking Englishmen to make of 'I will drown and nobody shall save me'? The implication here is of course that he was determined to drown and equally determined that nobody should try to save him.

Perhaps a rather rough and ready guide (though even here one hesitates to be dogmatic) is to regard 'should' and 'shall' as carrying some obligation, and to regard 'would' and 'will' as implying some determination. Hence, 'I will take lunch at one o'clock and at three I shall call round to see my nephew'. In other words, I have made up my mind to lunch at one, and I feel some kind of obligation to see my nephew at three.

The use of these words is perhaps better left to one's individual use and taste. Both 'shall' and 'will' can be interchangeably used to express the future tense: 'I will mend my boots'; 'I shall mend my boots'. The word 'shall' is now most frequently used in questions, such as, 'Shall I open the window?', and in commands, such as, 'You shall not kill', or, 'Members shall not transfer their fishing permit'. In those examples, 'will' would be inadequate because it only has the denotation of future tense, so it would sound like a prophecy: 'Members will not transfer their fishing permit'. For those interested in the distinctions between 'shall' and 'will', a useful guide may be seen from the following:

You *shall* have it tomorrow	– a promise (or threat!)
You *should* do this!	– a command, obligation
He *will* do it	– insists on it, (or a prophecy)
He *would* do it	– insisted on doing it

One thing is certain: 'should' and 'would' should not be mixed with 'shall' and 'will' in the same sentence. It is incorrect to say 'I *should* be glad if you *will* come to supper tonight'. 'I *should* be glad if you *would* come...', or, 'I *shall* be glad if you *will* come...' are correct.

'STOOD' AND 'SAT'

It is inexcusable to say, 'I'd like to speak to that girl who was *stood* over there'. Similarly, it is just as erroneous to say, 'The boy who's *sat* on that chair looks very like my brother'.

In these cases, the words 'was' and 'is' (auxiliary verbs) are followed by the participles 'standing' or 'sitting'. The habit of using 'sat' and 'stood' in their wrong senses is as logically absurd as saying, 'I'd like to see the girl who was *sang* (instead of 'singing') at the microphone.'

As with 'lie' and 'lay', perhaps the forms of 'stood' and 'sit' are best presented for memory in a table:

Finite form	Participle form	Past tense form
to sit: (I) sit	(I was) sitting	(I) sat
to stand: (I) stand	(I was) standing	(I) stood

'THAT KIND...'

'Kind' is a singular word and should not be preceded by 'those', unless of course it appears in the plural ('those kinds'). It is not logical to say that we do not care for 'those kind of people'. 'Kind', being singular, should be preceded by 'that'. We should say either, 'I do not care for *those kinds* of people', or, 'I do not care for *that kind* of person'.

'THE REASON WAS THAT...'

It would be incorrect to say,

The reason I am late is *because* I missed my train.

The word 'because' implies that there will be some further explanation beyond what I really did; it implies the creation of yet another clause to follow. For example, 'The reason I am late is, because I missed my train. I also missed the connecting coach'. In the example above, 'because' acts as a substitute for the word 'that':

The reason I am late is *that* I missed my train.

(It is simpler, of course, to omit the opening phrase 'The reason' and to simply say, 'I am late because I missed my train'.)

THE SPLIT INFINITIVE* (see footnote on next page)

A split infinitive is the insertion of an adverb between the preposition 'to' and the verb. 'To boldly go' from *Star Trek* is an example, as is 'to loudly speak'. The words 'boldly ' and 'loudly' are both adverbs, and 'to go' and 'to speak' are infinitive verb forms. These are rather awkward phrases, and it is because of its inelegance that the split infinitive would be best avoided in those cases.

On the other hand, there are many instances when the split infinitive adds more force to what has been said, as in:

We are going to strongly advise our opponents that this sort of thing must cease.

Strict grammarians might say that this is wrong, but where else can you place the adverb 'strongly'? To place it anywhere else seems artificial and ineffective. If the sentence had read, 'We are going to advise our opponents strongly...', then something, some forcefulness, would have been lost. And so would something of the naturalness be lost if we were to write, 'We are going strongly to advise our opponents...'.

Similarly, where would one put 'carelessly' in the following?

Do you mean to carelessly destroy all my carefully-laid plans?

I think that one must agree that from the point of view of forceful prose, it is better to leave 'carelessly' just where it is. If a lady were asked to dance, she might respond, 'I would prefer to not dance'. By placing the adverb 'not' where she has, it seems that she has focused on her expressed desire of not dancing, which might be more of a rebuff than if she had said, 'I would prefer not to dance', which might indicate that she might prefer to do something else instead.

Therefore, we naturally place the adverb in the position which will create the most impact for our purpose and context. A safe guide is to leave the split infinitive alone in cases where the adverb is causing its most intensifying value. If you listen out for occasions of the split infinitive, it is certain that you will find some occurrences where it is better style and meaning to leave the adverb just where it is.

The main trouble with this rule is that those who are over-conscious of it will place the adverb in a position that renders the

---

*The rule against the split infinitive derives from the pseudo-rules of certain grammarians in the eighteenth century who wanted to try to make English conform to Latin, which they saw as being orderly and therefore appropriate as a model for other languages. Their fault concerning the split infinitive, though, was that Latin infinitives consist of only one word (as they do in Greek, Hebrew, French and many other languages), so it is not possible for them to be split. English infinitives, most often (though not always) consisting of two words ('to witness', 'to translate', 'to walk' and so on), can be split and, therefore, provide a greater richness of possibilities than Latin. Sometimes, as well, English infinitives consist of a single word ('I watched her *walk* away' – finite verb 'watched', so 'walk' is infinitive; and in 'I can throw', the word 'throw' is infinitive – compare 'I am able to throw'), so any additional adverb could be inserted either side of 'walk' (I watched her walk silently away'). English cannot be controlled by any Latin model – and why should it be?

---

sentence weakened and inelegant, merely for the sake of some artificial rule whose inventor we may not care to respect. For example, 'It is our duty, my friends, for us all to acknowledge this gift gratefully and to applaud our benefactor wholly.' True, the writer of good English could have put the whole thing in a simpler and more concise manner, but the person at pains to avoid the split infinitive at all costs is often guilty of stooping to contrive some rather grim and unattractive evasions. That sentence seems to sound so much more natural and to have more force when it is recast as, 'It is our duty, my friends, for us all to gratefully acknowledge this gift and to wholly applaud our benefactor.'

Nevertheless, it is, I think, fair to say that the split infinitive can itself also create some ugly-sounding phrases, such as, 'I am sure Ann is going to delightfully sing', instead of, 'going to sing delightfully'. In the majority of instances the split infinitive might be better avoided. But we must always bear in mind that there are other occasions when the avoidance of it is unnecessarily pedantic.

The best rule is to be guided by style – how does it sound? – rather than strict observance of any Latin-based pseudo-rule.

'UNIQUE'

'Unique' has no qualifying comparatives or superlatives. If a thing is unique it is the only one of its kind. Therefore we should not speak of a thing, or person, as being 'more unique' than any other, nor being 'the most unique'. It is simply unique, standing on its own.

'WHERE' FOR 'WHEN'

It is worth remembering that 'where' refers to a place, and 'when' to time. Sometimes we read or hear, 'I cannot forget the occasion *where* we were soaked by the incoming tide'. The place and the time have become interchanged. It is better to say, 'I cannot forget the occasion *when* we were soaked', or, 'I cannot forget the beach *where* we were soaked.'

'WOULD HAVE' FOLLOWED BY A FURTHER 'HAVE'

In the sentence, 'I would have been the first to have offered a donation', the second 'have' is irrelevant and does not convey exactly what is intended. To have 'offered' implies that my action would have taken place some time previously. The correct version will make this clearer: 'I would have been the first to offer a donation'. Omit the second 'have', as in, 'She would have been the first girl to win the tennis club trophy' (not 'have won').

'WOULD OF' INSTEAD OF 'WOULD HAVE'

This error also occurs with 'could' and 'should'. We often hear,

He *would of* made a mistake.
He *could of* made a mistake.
He *should of* told someone.

These are typical of the highly unattractive Estuary English, and should be avoided. They should be corrected as,

He *would have* made a mistake.
He *could have* made a mistake.
He *should have* told someone.

This is an example of careless speech which can often creep into written passages. The word 'of' is a preposition, usually denoting possession ('the concordance of mine'), so has no place in a verb construction such as 'He would have made'. The word 'have' here is an auxiliary verb which is helping to define the tense being expressed.

TEST YOURSELF

Here are some 'Test Yourself' exercises which are based on the subject of this chapter. The task is to insert the missing word, or words. You may need to read back over some of the sections.

1. The Australian cricket team is being acclaimed better than – – team in the world.

2. The disciples shared the bread and fish – the hungry crowd.
3. If I –, I'll complete the manuscript by Friday.
4. Please, Sir, – I leave early?
5. This team doesn't all – – you, you know.
6. The concepts of the Reformation painters were – – those of the Renaissance painters.
7. If I – able, I'd love to cycle again.
8. There seem to be – plants in Jodie's garden this year.
9. I wouldn't say Eddie sings – his father could.
10. He – liked her poems, – her ideas behind them.
11. He quite accepts that he isn't one of the best captains who – led the team.
12. David had scarcely driven out of the forecourt – the noise started up again.
13. He thought he would rather like to talk to that girl – by the window.
14. The football manager made it quite clear that he wasn't going to tolerate – – of player.
15. If only you had bothered to ask, I could – easily done it for you.

Chapter 10

A SPOTLIGHT ON WORDS
WHICH OFTEN CAUSE DIFFICULTY

The English language is probably the richest in the world. Indeed, it is so rich and varied in its vocabulary that it is not surprising to find many words either misspelt or misplaced, especially when words of similar pronunciation are nearly spelled the same. Below is a list of words which often present difficulty.

Adverse: Contrary to, a set-back. 'The critic was full of adverse criticism of (was hostile to) the play.'

Averse: Opposed to, unwilling. 'I am averse to the idea of a hotel holiday.'

Affect: Verb meaning to act upon or influence. 'I cannot see how that will affect the outcome.'

Effect: Verb and noun. 1) Verb meaning to bring about or produce. 'He wanted to effect changes at the office.' 2) It is also a noun meaning the result of an action. 'The effect of his presence was to introduce fear and loathing in the team.'

All right: Frequently written as 'alright', although purists insist that the correct use is in two words, which I suppose has some sense as it is meaning to say that *all* is *right*. But there seems little purpose or sense in making any objection to 'alright'.

Allusion: To make an indirect reference to something. 'When I speak of celery I allude to your favourite food,' so, 'I made an allusion to celery.'

Illusion: A trick of sight, an optical illusion. 'The Indian rope-trick is thought to be an illusion.'

Allusive:	Making an indirect reference to something. Containing a reference to something.
Elusive:	Hard to find, difficult to trace, being evasive.
Illusive:	Having the quality of deceptiveness, illusion.
As long as:	Should be used for comparisons in measurements. 'The table was as long as the sofa.'
So long as:	If, on condition [that], only if, provided[that]. Used for conditions. 'Come round at eight, so long as you have done your homework.'
Canvas:	Cloth used for making sails, tents, etc., or for painting on.
Canvass:	To solicit support for a campaign, new venture or votes.
Eminent:	Of high degree, distinguished. 'Mark Twain is an eminent writer.'
Imminent:	Liable to take place very soon. 'We were in imminent danger of being flooded.'
Formally:	Something done with due regard for standard behaviour. 'He was formally introduced to the Queen,' or 'The Mayor was formally elected.'
Formerly:	That which obtained before. 'Lord Beaconsfield, formerly Disraeli, read very widely,' or 'Rod Laver was formerly the Wimbledon tennis champion.'
Hoard:	As a verb, to amass something, often money, or to collect and store away, as a miser does. As a noun, the store of treasure already accumulated.
Horde:	Noun, a band of people – 'a horde of savages' – a tribe in mass.
Industrial:	Adjective related to industry, describing the vicinity or concept of industry (factories). 'Birmingham is an industrial city.'
Industrious:	Busy activity, hard-working. 'The ant is an industrious insect.'

Licence:	The noun: a dog licence, a driving licence, permit, etc.
License:	The verb: to allow or grant a permit, hence the notice 'Licensed to sell tobacco and spirits.'
Lightening:	With the 'e', becoming less heavy: 'lightening the load'. Also, making less dark: 'the clouds on your picture need lightening'.
Lightning:	An electrical phenomenon in the sky (streak of lightning), followed by thunder.
Passed:	An action word, from the verb to pass. 'I have passed my driving test.' 'It seemed that summer passed quickly this year.'
Past:	A describing (descriptive), non-action word. 'Your past record is a good one.' 'It's long past your bed-time.'
Practice:	The noun – 'I must allow myself at least an hour's piano practice'; 'the doctors' practice'.
Practise:	The verb – 'Christopher is going to practise his tennis shots'; 'You should practise for an hour a day', or, 'practising doctors'.
Principal:	The main or chief figure or part, the head of a school or college. 'The principal source for the argument was your brother's opinion.'
Principle:	A fundamental truth, the right law, rule, axiom. A 'moral principle' or 'man of principle'.
Providing:	Giving. A participle form of the verb 'to provide'. Sometimes incorrectly used instead of 'provided that'.
Provided [that]:	If,[1] on condition [that], only if, so long as. 'You can go provided that you tell your mother.'

[1] Fowler and Fowler suggest, 'Provided is a small district in the kingdom of if, it can never be wrong to write if instead of provided: to write provided instead of if will generally be wrong, but is now and then an improvement in precision' (The King's English, Third Edition, 1931, p. 23).

Stationary: Something not moving, immobile. 'A stationary car.'

Stationery: With the 'e' it means writing paper, envelopes, etc.

Yoke: A wooden cross-piece made to fit the shoulders and support buckets, or to join oxen.

Yolk: The yellowish part of an egg.

TEST YOURSELF

Supply the missing words from those previously given.

1. We had gathered at the nets for some cricket –.
2. If you did not see the wheels of my car move, how can you say that the vehicle was not – .
3. A puppy has to be a certain age before it is necessary to take out a – for it.
4. It is a matter of – that one should pay debts promptly.
5. Thomas Hardy, one of the most – of English novelists, died in 1928.
6. The worker bee, always so active and – , is a fascinating creature to watch.
7. He spent many hours trying to – support for his cause.
8. I thought I saw a mirage, but can only assume that it was an optical –
9. A – of excited, yelling boys burst into the shop.
10. I am not exactly – to your going to France; it is simply that I must treat your plans with caution.
11. The roof was in – danger of collapsing as the flames spread higher.
12. Steaton House, – owned by the Dumark family, is now owned by the National Trust.
13. We couldn't be sure what – the weather would have on the race.
14. His contribution is unlikely to – the outcome.
15. The management would be disappointed not to – the restructuring this winter.
16. The others' jumps were not – – – those of Jonathan Edwards.
17. I'll mow the lawn tomorrow, – it will still be dry.
18. To prepare his students for their examination, the lecturer issued them – papers.

---

19. After her seventh attempt, Nora – her driving-test.
20. Only by – his panniers could the cyclist manage the hills.
21. They say – only strikes once.
22. Edwards should win the triple-jump, – – – he puts in his usual training.
23. It's not only children who dip bread in egg –.

WORDS OFTEN SPELT (SPELLED) INCORRECTLY

Past tenses of 'occur', 'prefer', 'refer' and so on, take on the ending 'red'. We have, therefore, 'occurred', 'preferred' and 'referred'. Do not overlook the double 'r'. Other words that sometimes give difficulty are:

accommodation: 'double 'c' and double 'm'.

budgerigar: remember the 'd' before the 'g'.

column, solemn: remember the ending of 'n'.

conscience, conscious, conscientious: 'c' after 's'.

disappointment, disappear: one 's' and double 'p'.

embarrassment: double 'r' and double 's'.

gauge: 'u' immediately after 'a'.

misspelt: double 's'.

necessary: one 'c' and double 's'.

occasion: double 'c' and single 's'.

persuasion: 'u' immediately after 's'.

precede: unlike proceed or succeed has no double 'e'. Likewise accede, recede, supersede.

queue: 'ue', 'ue' in quick succession.

rhythm: 'hy' before the 't'.

toboggan: one 'b' and double 'g'.

POINTS TO REMEMBER

Which words, ending in 'o', take on the plural suffixes of either 's' or 'es'? It is useful to know that words associated with music take the plural ending of 's' (because they are borrowed from Italian), while others take on 'es'. Hence:

alto	altos
cello	cellos
piano	pianos
soprano	sopranos

but:

halo	haloes
hero	heroes
potato	potatoes
tomato	tomatoes

'I' BEFORE 'E' EXCEPT AFTER 'C'

This rule has been a guide to generations. So we have:

believe

field

friend

niece

reprieve

sieve

But there are exceptions:

beige

seize

their

vein

weir

weird

Except after 'c' we also have of course:

deceive

perceive

receive

Chapter 11

PUNCTUATION

Practising writers rarely have to ponder over punctuation. Their use of it comes as naturally as the falling leaves. They know as if by instinct when to pause, mark time or come to a halt. By doing so, of course, they make their intentions clear. Indeed one may say that the sole purpose of punctuation is to make life easier for the readers, for it helps them to understand all the more plainly what the writer has in mind.

No doubt the majority of readers are already aware of what the various signs and symbols stand for, and will know too how to employ them, though it may not be without interest if we bring some refreshment to the memory and, at the same time, see how the misuses of punctuation can completely alter the meaning of a sentence.

The main purpose of this chapter, however, is to give a complete explanation of all the punctuation signs that you are ever likely to use.

THE FULL-STOP (.)

This sign is placed at the end of a sentence when the writer has stated all he wants to say about the subject. So:

Harry Danish galloped his black and white horse over the hills.

Here the writer has told us, for the time being at least, all he wants us to know about Harry Danish. (Incidentally, it is useful to know that the *subject* of a sentence is the person or thing that 'performs' the verb. In this instance, it was Harry Danish who 'galloped' his horse.)

If the writer had wanted to say more about Harry Danish, he could have put such information in parenthesis, that is, between commas like this:

Harry Danish, a very fine rider, galloped his black and white horse over the hills.

Or again, even further information could have been added (if the writer had wished to add it) by the use of a conjunction: 'although', 'and', 'because', 'but', 'unless', 'while' and so on. So:

Harry Danish, a very fine rider, galloped his black and white horse over the hills and did not dismount until he came within sight of the sea.

It is sometimes desirable, however, to introduce an entirely new subject (another 'performer' of the verb) into the same sentence. This is yet another instance of extending the sentence by use of the conjunction. For example:

Harry Danish, a very fine rider, galloped his black and white horse over the hills while Anne watched him with some admiration.

Here again, the writer has given all the information he deems necessary about his two subjects, Harry Danish and Anne. He therefore ends with a full-stop.

By way of a refresher, the reader may like to insert the full-stops and capital letters into this unpunctuated passage. The punctuated version appears in the Answers section at the end of the book.

there have been times in my life when i have felt in dire need of a holiday the family and i had often spent ten days or so in Cornwall where one may either lie on the beach and sunbathe or else go for long walks along delightful coastline Janet however thought she would like to explore the Lake District she said she had been keen to go to the Wordsworth area ever since she had discovered his poem *Tintern Abbey* some two years ago we discussed the matter for several days without coming to an agreement

in the end we decided to go to Ludlow in Shropshire i

**am not sure how we came to decide on Ludlow it was
perhaps because the area on a map looked so unspoilt
whatever the reason we all made up our minds to go to
this previously unexplored territory i must confess we
were impressed**

To repeat, then, the full-stop is used when the full meaning of what
the writer has to say has come to completion. Each new sentence
starts with a capital letter.

THE COMMA (,)

The comma has been described as a brief pause between groups of
words. That is exactly what it is. Some people overwork the comma
and use it where there should be a full-stop, as in, 'I might have
known you'd be late, you always are when you know I'm in a hurry'.
The comma is to be used only when we want to make a slight pause,
or if we wish to insert some extra information or another clause or
phrase into a sentence. For example, if we use the sentence, 'I first
met Thompson at the National Gallery in the autumn of last year', we
may want to say a little more about him, and therefore could say:

**I first met Thompson, an eminent landscape artist, at the
National Gallery in the autumn of last year.**

Just observe for a moment what the omission of a comma after the
word 'artist' would have conveyed to the reader. It would have
meant that Thompson was an eminent artist *at* the National Gallery
– which is not exactly what we meant to imply. Having stated that he
was an eminent artist at the National Gallery, I would have had to
carry on and say also where it was that I met him.

The comma is also used (provided that we consider such a brief
pause necessary) when we extend the sentence with another clause
by means of a conjunction, 'although', 'and', 'because', 'but',
'unless' and so on. For example:

I first met Thompson, an eminent landscape artist, in the

National Gallery in the autumn of last year, although it was some time before I recognized him.

We also use commas to mark off items in a list:

I bought pens, ink, paper, a box of disks and a ruler.

You will notice that there is no need to insert a comma after the word 'disks' because it is joined to the final word 'ruler' by the conjunction 'and' (although some writers might also insert commas in such cases). If the final word, however, is not joined by a conjunction, then the insertion of a comma is necessary. We may wish to produce a staccato effect (called asyndeton, or asyndetic) by writing:

She was witty, humorous, elegant, pretty, coy.

You will have gathered by now, of course, that it is the writer who dictates the careful functions of punctuation.

THE SEMI-COLON (;)

If you wish your reader to pause longer than a comma would cause, then you are fairly safe to use the semi-colon – a kind of midway break between the comma and the full-stop. It generally separates clauses (a clause is a group of words with a finite verb). There are certain additions to a sentence that we feel may not justify a full-stop, nor would it be correct to insert such a slight pause as the comma:

He did not arise very cheerfully on that April morning; perhaps he was still reminded of his dreams during the night.

You will see that the writer did not want us to pause so abruptly as a full-stop would have indicated, for his awakening uncheerfully on an April morning has a direct bearing on his dreams. On the other hand, what follows this semi-colon is a second clause, and it is not the comma's job to separate clauses. Indeed, a comma would have been quite wrong. There is nothing better, however, than another example to show where the semi-colon is used to its best effect, to demarcate clauses in a list:

Spring had burst like a tiny bomb. The early bees were about their business; birds, perched on tree-tops, sang at dawn; daffodils appeared; the girls, giggling in new dresses, took on a new appearance. Everything came alive.

The writer here wants you to take time to consider all the effects of spring. He wants to create a longer pause than a comma would provide, so he uses semi-colons. They are distinct from the commas which demarcate extra information inside the clauses.

THE COLON (:)

The colon is used for contradictions, illustrations and lists.

For contradictions, it is placed between statements when the latter half would seem to be a contradiction of the former. For instance:

Speech is silver: silence is golden.

A woman commands: a mere man nods but goes his own way.

For illustrations, the colon is also used when the second half of the whole sentence illustrates or exemplifies the first half, as in:

My friend Hargreaves invariably arrived late for every-thing: he appeared, as usual, just in time to see the guests depart.

My circumstances were different from what they had been: I was now a married man with a home of my own.

In *The Times* (*Play* section), there appeared this comment: 'One thing at least seems beyond doubt. Shakespeare captured exactly the young Prince Hal's turbulent relationship with his father'. Since the second sentence is an illustration of the first, it would have been appropriate to use a colon after the word 'doubt':

One thing at least seems beyond doubt: Shakespeare captured exactly the young Prince Hal's turbulent relationship with his father.

For lists, the colon is employed when there follows a list of people, places or things, for example:

He emptied his fishing-basket and there on the table lay the following: three hooks, a line, several flies, a reel and a rainbow trout.

THE POINTER (:–)

You may also come across a sign that looks like this :–

People sometimes wonder what this colon followed by a dash is called. It is, in fact, called the pointer, though its use is exactly the same as the colon. But since the colon is also used when there are lists of things that follow, the pointer need never be employed at all within the text. Use it if you wish, but the colon fulfils exactly the same purpose. It is useful, though, for introducing indented sections after a sentence requiring a question mark.

THE QUESTION MARK (?)

This mark is easy to employ. Simply, it is placed after a question, as in:

Is it true that you have three brothers?

Notice how the absence of a question mark can change a question into a statement, and the addition of one can change a statement into a question. Examples:

'You have two daughters?'
'You have two daughters.'

'You don't know,' said the barrister.
'You don't know?' said the barrister.

THE EXCLAMATION MARK (!)

Use it after any remark that implies force, such as exclamations, shouting, strong commands or humour, such as:

'Come here!' shouted the irate man.

'On my word!' said the professor as his opponent won the chess match.

'Mind your heads!' shouted the tree-feller.

'Hey! Cut that out!'

'Up with this I will not put!' (from Winston Churchill)

A note here: do not use the exclamation mark too often, otherwise the emphasis you intend will be lost by overuse.

THE DASH (–) AND HYPHEN (-)

The dash is a convenient form of punctuation, for it can be used for an afterthought either in the middle or at the end of a sentence. Provided it is not over-used, its usefulness lies in the fact that even the full flow of a sentence may be interrupted by it. Here are some examples:

There we all sat at those Christmas dinners – and what feasts they were – while outside the snow piled deeper and deeper.

In those days – and I was not quite sixteen at the time – it was possible to travel abroad with twenty pounds in one's pocket.

We found her wandering alone in the snow – and a wistful-looking creature she was.

We came across the house from out of the mists – and a gaunt, eerie building it appeared.

Word-processors and their printers mostly use the same symbol [-] for a dash or a hyphen, so we should note that a dash is longer than a hyphen in printed publications, when used for the examples above.

INVERTED COMMAS, QUOTATION MARKS OR SPEECH MARKS

Inverted commas are used when we wish to separate the words actually spoken by someone from what is often called *Reported Speech*, or *Indirect Speech*. Examples are:

Terry said he was due to arrive in Paris at noon. (Reported speech)
'I am due to arrive in Paris at noon,' said Terry. (Direct speech)

It is important to notice that inverted commas are placed only around words actually spoken; never, of course, around the speaker, nor around the reporting verbs ('said', 'remarked', 'shouted' etc.). Note also that inverted commas can be used to separate the spoken words from the speaker, even in the middle of a sentence. So:

'I decided long ago that I would never go to Lyme Regis again,' remarked Betty wistfully, 'though of course I would like to see Richard again.'

Observe too how the omission of speech marks can completely alter the meaning of a sentence:

'Your father,' said Mr Cranstone, 'is a very remarkable man.'
Your father said Mr Cranstone is a very remarkable man.

My uncle said the local postman is a talented musician.
'My uncle,' said the local postman, 'is a talented musician.'

Perhaps the most successful way of learning how to use speech marks correctly is to study an example, and then to ask yourself why some remarks are in inverted commas while others are not. For instance:

'I was not at my best on Friday morning,' remarked Mr Daniels ruefully.
He fidgeted a little uneasily and then in a confiding manner leaned across the table.

65

'The fact is,' he said – and here he hesitated – 'the fact is, I had been to a party the night before. And do you know what time I arrived home?'

He looked around him as if half-expecting to find an eavesdropper at his elbow.

'I arrived home at four o'clock in the morning.'

I did not consider his confession to warrant such secrecy, though out of politeness I could not very well tell him so.

'Did you really?'

'Yes,' he sighed. 'What do you think of that, eh?'

I did not know what to think.

QUOTATION MARKS AROUND TITLES – ARE THEY NECESSARY?

It used to be the custom to place titles of books, plays, films and songs within quotation marks, though it seems that this custom is fast disappearing. In written passages such titles should appear in italics.

Since word-processors have the facility for italics, there should be little difficulty in following that procedure. For those writers still using typewriters, it is best to underline titles (which is the copy-editor's mark for italics in any case). Hand-written scripts can employ the same underlining procedure.

There are some instances when inverted commas are used, for the titles of papers quoted from learned journals for example, and in references or bibliographies, but these need not confuse the issue at this stage. Stick with italics or underlining and your reader will know what you mean.

TEST YOURSELF

You may like to insert the inverted commas where you think they are necessary in the following passage. The corrected version is in the

Give me your hand and I will tell your fortune, said Aunt Martha. She smiled at David benignly. David was reluctant to decline though he had long been sceptical of pastimes that pretended to foretell the future. I'll let you tell my hand, said David, on one condition. Oh indeed! said Aunt Martha. And what condition is that? The condition, said David, is that you do not tell me anything that might give me a sleepless night. Aunt Martha laughed. Have I ever told you anything that caused you needless worry? David had to confess that she hadn't. Well that's all right then, replied Aunt Martha. What are you worrying about? I suppose there's nothing to worry about, answered David. But there's a simple explanation for that. And what, laughed his aunt, is that? It was David's turn to laugh. Because, he said, you've never read my hand before.

Chapter 12

THE APOSTROPHE

A chapter on the use of the apostrophe has been included in this book of everyday English usage because, like punctuation, its misuse can often convey a different meaning from that which we intended.

There are some students of English who maintain that there are too many apostrophes in our language, that many of these vertical dashes or inverted commas could very well be omitted without loss of meaning, and that they slow down the rapid communication of words via computer or e-mail. George Bernard Shaw refused to be bothered with apostrophes in contracted words such as 'dont', 'shant', 'couldnt' and 'wouldnt', and we must admit that these omissions didn't in the least detract from the meaning of the words. Shaw, though, was a law to himself, and we would probably – and justifiably so – be accused of slap-dash, hurried writing if we were to copy him. So for ordinary people like you and me, it is probably better to remain loyal to customary usage. In any case, omissions in some contexts could cause embarrassing difficulties: 'cant', 'hell', 'id', 'its', 'shed', 'shell', 'wed', 'well'.

Moreover, there are some instances where the omission of an apostrophe would cause a good deal of confusion. Consider, for example:

The dogs bones.

I wonder who could say how many dogs there are supposed to be? One, or more than one? Similarly, consider 'the girls costumes', 'the boys fishing-rods', 'the soldiers rations'. One possessor, or more? It is impossible to say. Perhaps this is a convenient point to look at, shall we say, the Rules for the apostrophe and its uses.

RULE NUMBER 1

The apostrophe is used to signify possession. We write of Mary's hat, the carpenter's bench, our neighbour's garden. Notice (and I must apologize if, for some, this appears too elementary) that the apostrophe is placed before the 's' only when one person is the possessor. It is placed after the 's' when more than one are the possessors.

It is here that we refer again to the 'dogs bones'. In the first example below we see that there is one dog; in the second there are more.

The dog's bones.
The dogs' bones.

RULE NUMBER 2

Remember, however, that in words which already have a plural meaning, the apostrophe is still placed before the 's' – just as if the word were singular.

The children's toys.
The women's waiting-room.
The men's fishing-rods.

It should also be observed that in singular words which end in 's', we often add another 's' after the apostrophe. We do this for the sake of smoother sound: it is the way we speak.

St James's Church.
The Prince of Wales's paintings.
The Jones's shed.
The Sparkes's garden.

RULE NUMBER 3

The other common use of the apostrophe (disregarded by Shaw) occurs when a letter has been omitted, words that we call *contractions* because two words have been contracted together:

can't, couldn't, could've, didn't, don't, hasn't, haven't, he'd, he'll, he's, I'd, I'll, I'm, it's, it'll, I've, isn't, mightn't, might've, she'd, she'll, she's, shouldn't, should've,

they'd, they're, they've, wasn't, we'd, we'll, we're, weren't, we've, who'd, who'll, who's, won't, wouldn't, would've, you'd, you'll, you're, you've.

Similar to the contraction is the *elision*, when a letter or number of letters have been omitted from a word. The apostrophe is used to replace the missing element. These appear most frequently in older poetry and hymns. Common examples are 'o'er' for 'over', 'H'ven' for 'Heaven'.

RULE NUMBER 4

Sometimes the names of two people are linked together, such as 'John and Mary'. Both John and Mary might possess the same thing – but against whose name do we place the apostrophe? When speaking, it would perhaps be unnecessarily pedantic to use the apostrophe twice in such an example as 'This is John's and Mary's house'. We therefore put the apostrophe on the last-mentioned:

This is John and Mary's house.
On this site they are going to build Foster and Brown's shop.

COMMON ERRORS WITH THE APOSTROPHE

It is as well to be aware of two common errors.

The first concerns 'it's' and 'its'. These are two very different words, the first one meaning 'it is', and the second referring to the possessive adjective similar to 'mine', 'her', 'our', 'his', 'their' or 'your'.

It's quite clear that you are not going to go.
The bird was building its nest.
It's got its bones.

The second error, occurring more often in speech, is apparent in 'I am a friend of Mary's'. Mary's who, or what? There is obviously no need at all for the apostrophe, and the sentence should read:

I am a friend of Mary.
or, I am Mary's friend.

TEST YOURSELF
Insert the apostrophes where necessary.

1. Todays news of the four Everest climbers feat made good reading.
2. Its time we received a visit from the Cooksons cat.
3. The babies prams are displayed in Jones & Browns window.
4. They say a ghost used to walk in St Peter and Pauls churchyard.
5. The squirrel is gathering its nuts.
6. The childrens stories are to be found in the Young Peoples department of the library.
7. We walked by St James Church and found the Robinsons already waiting for us.
8. These books are yours but Marys books are here.
9. I dont mind where you go so long as you avoid the girls playground.
10. My horses name is Silver King, but I understand that the Robinsons horses are always named after their owner.

Chapter 13

REVISION

The following revision exercises are to help you test yourself on the various topics covered throughout this book. The answers are in the Answers section at the end of the book.

EXERCISE A

Seven of the following nine sentences are wrong:

1. Jack Spring, who you saw dashing round the bend today, has to catch the 7.35 every morning.
2. The tramp had laid in the barn all night.
3. Leaning against the oak tree, I watched the lake in the moonlight.
4. It was kind of you to invite Joan and I to lunch.
5. She is as clever and much prettier that Molly.
6. Mr Crabtree, as well as his wife, were present at the ceremony.
7. She wore silver bracelets on her wrist, the value of which I do not know.
8. Mrs Perkins told her dog to lay down, but the dog did not obey.
9. Was this the tramp to whom you gave fifty pence?

EXERCISE B

Seven of the following nine sentences are wrong:

1. The newspaper boy was stood at the corner, shivering with cold.
2. I did not in the least mind them going so early.
3. It's clear enough that the winning of the game depends upon you and me.
4. Neither Jim nor Tom have ever played squash before.
5. I would like each man in this room to raise his right hand if he agrees with what I've said.
6. Mr Jackson's action, in refusing to let us cross his land, was the most unfriendliest action I have seen for some time.

7. My mother was rather alarmed at us staying out so late.
8. We were told by the fishermen that he had caught enough trout to share between five people.
9. I should be much obliged if you will return the book to me.

EXERCISE C
Six of the following eight sentences are wrong:

1. My sister has decided to do her hair like you do.
2. I cannot believe that your fast bowler is more speedier than Bill.
3. The stranger who came to the door turned out to be my Uncle Henry.
4. You say that this picture is almost priceless, but is it any more unique than the one by Leonardo da Vinci?
5. Was this the person who you saw fishing in the lake? (Would the omission of the relative pronoun 'who' really matter?)
6. I believe him to be one of the best tennis players who have ever played at Wimbledon.
7. Each person is asked to leave their hats and coats with the attendant.
8. He was sat on his chair by the fire all evening.

EXERCISE D
Five of the following eight sentences are wrong:

1. What is wrong with this sentence? Nothing, as far as I can see.
2. I feel sure you can run much faster than them.
3. The boy who received the prize with a gracious bow is sometimes apt to think himself a cut above the rest of us.
4. You going to Paris at Easter fits in perfectly with our plans.
5. If only you had asked she and I to come to your help all this trouble would have been avoided.
6. Of all our water birds I think the kingfisher is the most beautiful.
7. The lovers had lied by the forest glade in the moonlight.
8. Jumping over the fence on our new mare, my watch was entangled with the reins.

EXERCISE E

Six of the following seven sentences are wrong:

1. We did not and could not have known that the workmen were coming.
2. I do not like Jim wading in the deep water.
3. Feeling rather superior, we preferred not to associate ourselves with those kind of plans.
4. Of the two books I have here I believe this one to be the best.
5. I have seven keys here, but none of them are the right fit.
6. I will send for the employee whom I know is responsible for these petty disagreements.
7. These three parcels are heavy, I agree, but this one is the heaviest.

EXERCISE F

Eight of the following ten sentences are wrong:

1. I can't run like I used to.
2. The motorist, as well as the cyclist, were involved in the accident.
3. This is a different book to what I expected.
4. Leaning over the bridge, the fish swam in shoals below me.
5. None of these fishing-rods is going to be of much use for catching pike.
6. The reason I did not go to London was because I missed the train.
7. As a painter of the English countryside, Constable is unique.
8. I should not be surprised if it does not snow.
9. Tom King, who we chose to represent us, captained the side very well.
10. My uncle did not in the least mind us making such a noise.

EXERCISE G

Five of the following seven sentences are wrong:

1. Less men were hurt on the rugger field this season than last.
2. Climbing to the top of the hill, the sea lay below us.
3. He took up his paint brushes again just like he had always done.
4. There were fewer members of the club here tonight than at any other time.

5. It was plain that each player had suddenly lost their tempers.
6. 'Nobody, surely, could be more tolerant than I,' he said.
7. The way he chips a stone into something life-like is rather unique.

EXERCISE H
Six of the following eight sentences are wrong:
1. The lawn-mower, as well as the hosepipe, were very much in evidence.
2. None of the tools you have shown are of much use.
3. In swerving to avoid the dog, a lamp-post hit the bumper.
4. My uncle said that he agreed in principal with what had been done.
5. Dorothy is by far the slimmest of the two sisters.
6. Martin, accompanied by his dog, was the first to arrive.
7. You will find all you require at the stationary counter.
8. Was this the man to whom you gave the message?

EXERCISE I
Five of the following seven sentences are wrong:
1. I would not attempt to go over the mountain pass if I was you.
2. A great variety of musical pieces were played by the symphony orchestra.
3. The two old ladies appeared to be supporting each other along the busy pavement.
4. Mr Hardcastle has completed more crossword puzzles than any person in this competition.
5. The men had hardly finished painting the bridge than they were told to apply a second coat.
6. Had he accepted the post, Mr Dolly would have been the first man to have worn the new uniform.
7. It is the duty of us all to help one another.

ANSWERS TO TEST YOURSELF QUESTIONS

CHAPTER 1   BETWEEN YOU AND ME (Page 10)

1. correct
2. correct
3. incorrect – 'you and me'
4. correct
5. incorrect – 'you and me'
6. correct

CHAPTER 2   THE UNRELATED PARTICIPLE (Page 13)

1. Sitting on his horse, he saw the sea lying below him.
2. As I was jumping over the fence, my...
3. An oak-dressing table, newly-polished, for sale...
   OR: A newly-polished oak-dressing table, for sale...
4. Shake this medicine vigorously before...
5. She painted all day, and the picture...
6. Jane danced all over the ballroom floor, and her head...
7. As I cycled round the corner, the wheel fell off.

CHAPTER 3   'WHO' AND 'WHOM' (Page 15)

1. whom
2. who
3. whom
4. who
5. who
6. whom

CHAPTER 4   'SHE' AND 'I' – 'HER' AND 'ME' (Pages 19–20)

1. than I (do)
2. than she (is)
3. correct
4. he and I
5. correct
6. him and me
7. as high as she (could)
8. except her

CHAPTER 5   TAKING POSSESSION (Page 22)

1. The farmer did not mind their going...
2. correct
3. I have not the slightest objection to your...
4. I remember his asking me...
5. correct
6. We were all surprised at your...
7. ... by our arriving late (our late arrival)

CHAPTER 6   HOW TO BE LOYAL TO YOUR SUBJECTS (Page 28)

1. ... is too heavy
2. ... to place his vote
3. ... has yet scored over fifty
4. ... has accepted
5. ... should reconsider his decision

CHAPTER 6   ANOTHER WORD OR TWO ABOUT LOYALTY TO SUBJECTS (Page 28)

1. The Queen and the Duke were present...
2. ... and various other aspects of nature lore are necessary...
3. The electrician and his mate are going to install...
4. ... poems of Robert Frost were by his bed

CHAPTER 7   'MORE' AND 'MOST' (Page 31)

1. the more pretty *or* prettier
2. correct
3. most ugly *or* ugliest
4. more sad *or* sadder
5. correct
6. most accurate
7. correct

CHAPTER 8   'LIE' AND 'LAY' (Page 34)

1. lain
2. laying
3. lie
4. lie
5. laid
6. lying
7. lay
8. lain (or, been lying)

CHAPTER 9   OTHER COMMON ERRORS   (Pages 50–1)

1. any other
2. among
3. can
4. may
5. revolve around (or, centre on)
6. different from
7. were
8. fewer
9. as
10. neither... nor
11. have
12. when

13. sitting
14. that kind
15. have

CHAPTER 10   A SPOTLIGHT ON WORDS (Pages 55–6)

1. practice
2. stationary
3. licence
4. principle
5. eminent
6. industrious
7. canvass
8. illusion
9. horde
10. averse
11. imminent
12. formerly
13. effect
14. affect
15. effect
16. as long as
17. provided [that] (if, only if, so long as)
18. past
19. passed
20. lightening
21. lightning
22. so long as (if, only if, provided [that])
23. yolk

CHAPTER 11   THE FULL-STOP – CORRECTED AND PUNCTUATED VERSION (Pages 59–60)

There have been times in my life when I have felt in dire need of a holiday. The family and I had often spent ten days or so in Cornwall where one may either lie on the beach and sunbathe, or else go for long walks along delightful coastline. Janet, however, felt she would like to explore the Lake District. She said she had been keen to go to the Wordsworth area ever since she had discovered his poem *Tintern Abbey* some two years ago. We discussed the matter for several days without coming to an agreement.

In the end, we decided to go to Ludlow in Shropshire. I am not sure how we came to decide on Ludlow. It was, perhaps, because the area on a map looked unspoilt. Whatever the reason, we all made up our minds to go to this previously unexplored territory. I must confess we were impressed.

CHAPTER 11   INVERTED COMMAS – PUNCTUATED VERSION (Pages 66–7)

'Give me your hand and I will tell your fortune,' said Aunt Martha.

She smiled at David benignly. David was reluctant to decline though he had long been sceptical of pastimes that pretended to foretell the future.

'I'll let you read my hand,' said David, 'on one condition.'

'Oh, indeed!' said Aunt Martha. 'And what condition is that?'

'The condition,' said David, 'is that you do not tell me anything that might give me a sleepless night.'

Aunt Martha laughed.

'Have I ever told you anything that caused you needless worry?'

David had to confess that she hadn't.

'Well, that's all right then,' replied Aunt Martha. 'What are you worrying about?'

'I suppose there's nothing to worry about,' answered David. 'But there's a simple explanation for that.'

'And what,' laughed his aunt, 'is that?'

It was David's turn to laugh.

'Because,' he said, 'you've never read my hand before.'

CHAPTER 12   THE APOSTROPHE (Page 71)

1. Today's news of the four Everest climbers' feat... (more than one)
2. It's time we received a visit from the Cooksons' cat. (more than one Cookson)
3. The babies' prams are displayed in Jones & Brown's window.
4. ...St Peter and Paul's churchyard.
5. correct
6. The children's stories are to be found in the Young People's department.
7. We walked by St James's Church...
8. These books are yours but Mary's books are here.
9. I don't mind where you go so long as you avoid the girls' playground.
10. My horse's name is Silver King, but I understand the Robinsons' horses...

CHAPTER 13   ANSWERS TO REVISION QUESTIONS
EXERCISE A (Page 72)

1. 'whom' for 'who'
2. 'lain' for 'laid'
3. correct
4. Joan and me
5. She is as clever as and much prettier than...

6. was present
7. She wore silver bracelets, the value of which I do not know, on her wrist.
   OR: I do not know the value of the silver bracelets that she wore on her wrist.
   OR: On her wrist she wore silver bracelets, the value of which I do not know.
8. 'lie' for 'lay'
9. correct

EXERCISE B (Page 72)

1. 'standing' for 'stood'
2. 'their' for 'them'
3. correct
4. 'has' for 'have'
5. correct
6. 'most unfriendly' or 'the unfriendliest'
7. 'our' for 'us'
8. 'among' for 'between'
9. 'would' for 'will'

EXERCISE C (Page 73)

1. 'as' for 'like'
2. 'more speedy' or 'speedier'
3. correct
4. A thing is never *more* unique. But here the word must be replaced by something else – beautiful, wonderful, exquisite, etc.
5. 'whom' for 'who' (but the omission of 'whom' is more colloquial)
6. correct
7. 'his hat (or her) and coat' for 'their hats and coats'
8. 'sitting' for 'sat'

EXERCISE D (Page 73)

1. correct
2. 'they' for 'them'
3. correct
4. 'your' for 'you'
5. 'her and me' for 'she and I'
6. correct
7. lain
8. As I jumped over the fence on our new mare, my watch...

EXERCISE E (Page 74)

1. We did not know and could not have known...
2. 'Jim's' for 'Jim'
3. 'that' for 'those'
4. 'better' for 'best'
5. 'is' for 'are' (none means 'not one')
6. 'who' for 'whom'
7. correct

EXERCISE F (Page 74)

1. 'as' for 'like'
2. 'was' for 'were'
3. 'from' to 'to'
4. Sentence needs recasting. As I was leaning over the bridge, I saw the fish swimming in shoals.
5. correct
6. 'that' for 'because'
7. correct
8. double negative! I should not be surprised if it does snow (unless of course you really do mean that you would not be surprised if it does not snow).
9. 'whom' for 'who'
10. 'our' for 'us'

EXERCISE G (Page 74)

1. 'fewer' for 'less'
2. Climbing to the top of the hill, we saw...
3. 'as' for 'like'
4. correct
5. 'his temper' for 'their tempers'
6. correct
7. unique – never 'rather' unique

EXERCISE H (Page 75)

1. 'was' for 'were'
2. 'is' for 'are'
3. a lamppost does not swerve. Recast the sentence. Who was doing the swerving?
4. 'principle' for 'principal'
5. 'slimmer' for 'slimmest'
6. correct
7. stationery
8. correct

EXERCISE I (Page 75)

1. 'were' for 'was'
2. 'was' for 'were' ('variety' is singular)
3. correct
4. any other person
5. 'when' for 'than'
6. ...would have been the first man to wear the new uniform.
7. correct

AFTERWORD
ON STANDARD ENGLISH

WHAT IS STANDARD ENGLISH?

I should establish first what I mean by 'Standard English', for there is a considerable amount of agreement concerning which grammatical forms are accepted as standard.

For my own definition, I do not mean what I think Doctor Johnson meant: a preoccupation with prohibitions on split infinitives, opening sentences with the conjunctions 'and' or 'but', or closing them with prepositions. Nor do I mean prohibitions on intellectually useful additions and changes. I do, though, mean some prescriptions towards sophisticated aesthetic standardizations, especially concerning verb forms.

The word 'standard' can have two useful denotations for us: a norm, and a level of achievement. As a *norm*, we can refer to the English which is normally spoken and written by its educated users, by those who most care about language. Against this *norm*, we can readily identify other forms. As a *level of achievement*, we can refer to the English in which our books are written. Against this *level of achievement*, we can measure and evaluate other uses.

Examples of spoken standards would be those used by the Queen and the current Prime Minister Tony Blair. Examples of a written standard are found in most of our national newspapers. Standard English is also the written form of the law, politics, religion, education and other important institutions, and of most formal literature.

There is no doubt: the most highly educated aspire to the highest forms of language, and this inevitably means a form of Standard

English. Among the many great standard-bearers of the English language are the novelists Jane Austen and John Steinbeck:

It is a truth universally acknowledged, that a single man in possession of a good fortune, must be in want of a wife. *(Pride and Prejudice)*

To the red country and part of the grey country of Oklahoma the last rains came gently, and they did not cut the scarred earth. *(The Grapes of Wrath)*

The effect of the subordination, the balancing ('in possession of', 'in want of') and the rhythm of Austen; the fronted adverbial (To...Oklahoma'), the seamless compounding ('and...and') and the balancing ('came gently', 'did not cut') and the liquid fluency of Steinbeck: it seems wellnigh impossible to see how these could be improved in a single syllable.

WHERE DID STANDARD ENGLISH COME FROM?
The standardization of languages occurs in large and diverse societies, and is associated with a written form. Lesley Jeffries made this observation:

There are usually four stages in the establishment of a standard language. Firstly one dialect is chosen, secondly it has to be accepted by the powerful ruling and educated classes, thirdly its functions are extended to all the prestigious functions of education and government, and finally there are attempts to make the variety regular in its patterns and as stable as possible.
(The Language of Twentieth-Century Poetry,
Macmillan, 1993, p. 2)

The process, then, which Jeffries suggests is this:

1) a dialect is chosen;
2) a dialect is accepted by the ruling and educated;
3) the dialect is extended;
4) attempts are made to regularize the dialect.

When Geoffrey Chaucer (c.1340–1400) was writing his *Canterbury Tales* there was no such thing as Standard English. You could spell how you liked. And that is what people had to do. Even in texts of high literary status, the same word might be spelled in two or more different ways.

When printing was developed in the late fifteenth century, Standard English began to emerge as the conventional written form. The first book in English was printed in 1475 by William Caxton, in Bruges in Belgium. He established the first printing press in England in 1477.

In its earliest form, English is said to have developed from an old East Midland (an area including London, Oxford, Cambridge) dialect, gradually replacing the French and Latin which had been used for legal and official functions. With the printing of documents in law, commerce, government and literature, English society became more sophisticated and more complex, so there was a gradual process towards standardization. William Caxton mostly took up the conventions of this East Midland dialect, which was to become Standard English.

The equivalent happened in France when in 1650 the Académie Française was established, under the influence of courtly powers in Paris and Versailles. The Académie insisted that the French language be spelt and spoken in certain ways.

Back in England, as standards were institutionalized, sixteenth century printed and written texts began to look more like modern English. Although it was already occurring by the time William Tyndale was executed (1536), we see the pinnacle of this development towards our forms today in William Shakespeare's plays (said to be written between 1590 and 1611), and then in what has become known as *The Authorised Bible* (1611).

The most vigorous and conscious efforts to standardize written English were made in the eighteenth century. The works of three major figures formed a notable linguistic trinity: James Harris's *Hermes* (1751), Samuel Johnson's *Dictionary of the English Language* (1755), and Bishop Lowth's *A Short Introduction to English Grammar* (1762).

The well-known Dr Samuel Johnson (1709–84) was a lexicographer, critic, poet and conversationalist. Set down as a definition of people's speech, his dictionary fixed the English language for the first time. A service was done for English.

There were, though, unhelpful aspects of the three men's work. The worst was perhaps their unfortunate over-prescriptive attempts to align English with Latin: the concept of standardization was an attempt to model language on Latin because of its fixed rules. (They would have served us better if they had used as their model not Latin, but Greek and Hebrew, which are more flexible than Latin.) But those alignments with Latin do not always work. Also the stability of language was linked with social stability. Lowth had a hierarchical philosophy of language as a basis for his *Grammar*; he was concerned with making English more closely resemble classical languages. His *Grammar* was addressed to the already educated; his complex rules made language more difficult to learn. Refined language and vulgar language were even described as different languages with different etymologies, vocabularies and syntaxes, which, I suppose, is partly true (Latin and French against Anglo-Saxon). And Johnson's and Lowth's attitudes equated ignorance of Greek and Latin with immorality – a foolish equation. There is certainly no link between classical mythology and any notion of anything usefully moral, or righteous..

In the United States, the spelling of American English was both simplified and changed by Noah Webster in 1828, when his *American Dictionary* was published.

In England, revolution inevitably came in the form of new grammars and writing theories (such as Cobbett's *A Grammar of the*

English Language, 1819, and Paine's *Rights of Man*, 1791–92), together with their arguments that refined and vulgar languages are the same language.

Standard English became, and remains, the received, conventional English for one reason: consensus. And for about four hundred years since, the best users of English – its best writers – have found Standard English to be its most useful form for expressing their ideas to the greatest number; so have lawyers, teachers, businessmen, governments and friends exchanging letters. Nobody has invented a superior form of English, and, in my opinion, it is now unlikely that anybody will: possibly another as good, but not superior. If a new form were to be accepted, it might no longer be English.

ATTACKS AGAINST STANDARD ENGLISH

It is of course more or less true what some theorists have been saying recently: that Standard English is one version of English along with other dialects. There are also infinitesimal distinctions in varieties of Standard English (such as American, British, or South African English). However, some of these contemporary theorists have been making attempts to dislodge Standard English, despising it (in reverse snobbery) as a 'prestige dialect'. Their theories need not be taken seriously, because all their books are written in Standard English. Standard English – the so-called 'prestige dialect' which they would like to topple – is the only English in which those theorists have been able to communicate their ideas clearly to the greatest number.

When all their rhetoric is cast aside, we discover that a main element of these radicals' attacks against Standard English is their defence of aesthetically displeasing, irregular forms. In some extreme linguistic texts, their defence is made by uncritical inclusions (alongside educated speech) of teenagers' and uneducated users' speech (but not writing!) in their most unattractive and irregular forms, so elevating the status of those forms: expressions such as 'ennit' (isn't it), 'could of' (could have), 'should of' (should have), 'would of' (would have), 'is yuh' (are you), 'incha' (aren't you), 'I aren't' (I'm not), 'I've took' (I've taken), 'stood standing' (standing), 'dunnit' (doesn't it), 'I was sat' (I was sitting), 'I was stood' (I was standing), 'off of' (off), dropped aitches, for example ''Arry 'eld 'is 'ead 'igh' (Harry held his head high), double negatives such as 'I don't want nuffin' (I don't want anything), and 'ain't got no' (haven't got any). So they are taking their new standards from those speakers who have the very least knowledge of language, and the very least regard for it as well.

Anthony Burgess complained over ten years ago that 'every perversion of grammar is now regarded as a victory for democracy'.

One of those radical texts attacking Standard English attempts to justify as a dialect such non-standard spoken forms as 'I aren't going', 'me and him fixed it', 'he hurt hisself', 'she come back', 'we was stood', 'I see him yesterday' and 'that bloke what I knows'. (The writer of that text all but refuses to acknowledge anything as bad grammar or, more importantly for me, as aesthetically displeasing.) But that excuse falters on two counts. First, those are not a dialect, regional form, but are as widespread as Standard English; they are simply a non-standard form of poor, uneducated English. Now that's an entirely different matter from regional dialects which often have a charm all of their own. Second, language has aesthetic values, and there is absolutely nothing aesthetically pleasing about those poor forms. Some, perhaps, would be glad to be using those poor forms, because it would typecast them as hard or thuggish. Others, though – I know some – are glad to learn more pleasing forms in their speech and writing.

The great changes to English, when they have come, have been innovations and exquisite subtleties from mightily gifted writers: Geoffrey Chaucer, William Tyndale, William Shakespeare, Dr Johnson. There is no one today of such immense stature.

Why, then, do these modern (or post-modern) radical theorists not write in those unattractive forms which they seem to so admire? Even if we wanted to agree with them, we'd soon suffer the consequences if we were to write application forms, legal documents and examinations in some idiosyncratic and uneducated sounding form. If we hold no standards up for language, we might soon become unintelligible, barbaric. If we wish to keep producing literature of the highest stylistic calibre which can hold up its head with the world, it is the cultured forms of Standard English we should be extolling, not the sub-English of those who have the very least care and knowledge of it. All trades and professions aspire to standards; so should users of language.

DEFENCES AGAINST THE ATTACKS
An upholding of standards is a defence on behalf of sophistication and against barbarism. Soap opera and teenage cults of rebellious bar-barism and ugliness – yobspeak – are the bolshevization of language. However, there are a number of things which might be confused with a defence for Standard English. Establishing standards in a language is nothing to do with snobbery. Nor is it anything to do with dismissing regional dialects, which are a richness. Even those dialects can be found to have their own regular forms, which is the same thing as standardization. Nor is a standard anything to do with accents, another richness; many who speak with accents speak in Standard English. Nor is the notion of standards anything to do with morality. Language, most of all, shows character (as novelists know): 'Language most shows a man: Speak that I may see thee' (Ben Johnson). And there is such a thing as bad use of language, and, as well, bad language. Nor is a defence of standards a defence of time-wasting arguments about ending sentences with prepositions (which there is nothing wrong with). Nor is it any defence of English as an international language, at the expense of other languages (which is a tragedy).

No, one purpose behind the concept of a standard of a language is – or should be – so that it functions with the greatest possible clarity and scope; Standard English is not regionally orientated, so it is the most widely understood. Another purpose is so that it func-tions with the greatest possible aesthetic excellence, so its good users give pleasure to their listeners and readers. And out of that standard of excellence comes the best literature. Language has aesthetic values, as do poetry and music.

There is no reason to abandon Standard English; there is nothing better around.

The most obvious and sensible argument in favour of a form of Standard English is that there is nothing wrong with it. Those theorists attacking it, it seems, are attacking its users out of political spite and envy, or, at best, out of misguided ideas, rather than finding any shortcomings in the language.

I would like to extend Dr Jeffries's four processes in the selection of a dialect (which I cited at the beginning of this essay):

5) the dialect becomes a standard and stabilized form, permitting development, new words, and growth;
6) the dialect is attacked (by invaders, or for political reasons), sometimes for better, often for worse.

So our dialect of Standard English is currently under attack. This attack is for political reasons, not aesthetic or utility ones, and the attackers are not suggesting any replacement which is as good or as useful. It doesn't seem any more than a slump downwards towards the lowest common denominator – yet another marker in the descent of British culture.

It is utterly unthinkable that nations proud of the greatness of their literature and language, the ancient Hebrews, the Greeks, the Romans, would have written grammars drooling over and trying to justify the language forms of the very worst of its users.

TWO ATTACKS ANSWERED

One claim being made by the attackers is that Standard English spelling (orthography) is said to be out of date. Those radical reformers want to change English spelling to relieve themselves of difficulties over certain eccentric words. The reformers' argument is based on an assumption that English spelling is difficult. There are two arguments against that: first, this is an exaggeration; second, even if it is difficult, so what? It is true that English spelling is sometimes odd, but that is all part of its charm. However, the fault lies not in the language, but in our education system, which is unable (or unwilling) to teach school pupils how to spell with the same accuracy which former generations were able to attain. There are many superb schoolteachers; the fault lies not in them, but in the policies controlling them. There have been complaints in the media, and in the employment world, that even many university graduates now have a much lower standard of literacy than was achieved in past ages. I have witnessed for myself that this is true. Not so long ago, spelling and punctuation and grammar were taught by quite simple methods, and they were effective. Now we hear of immature objections to such teaching, because it is said to be associated with a former age of British history which the objectors do not like, preferring this post-modern one. But that is not a mature argument against teaching good forms of language, nor is it any argument about language.

It is not our spelling which is out of date, but our teaching methods and ideas which need to – not catch up – but catch *back* up with those which once equipped our school pupils and university graduates with a superior grasp of literacy than is generally being achieved today.

In any case, even if a new orthography were introduced, our current education methods and ideas still wouldn't equip pupils with a better achievement in literacy. They still wouldn't be able to spell. If they're not taught how to spell, what can they do? If they don't want to spell, they don't want to spell. If they can't spell, they can't spell. It wouldn't make any difference. Also, it's more than a matter of spelling: it's grammar and punctuation too.

Another prong of attack against normal English is the suggestion that the structure of language is changing – changing right under our very noses – wow! can't you see it? – it's exciting!!! This uninformed argument comes from the economical forms of language currently being used in electronic mail, the Internet and text messaging. The claims imply the change would be a good change.

The computer-world formats of language are elliptical for reasons of time and money. They are akin to the old telegram forms, typically omitting some grammatical functions and abbreviating spellings by removing vowels. This shorthand form is useful in its context. Away from that context, however, our ordinary uses of language would be extremely irritating and often incomprehensible if they became elliptical and abbreviated. Language structure depends on a range of particles which never pass away: conjunctions ('We want not stultified language, *but* clear language'), determiners ('We don't just want *any* grapes; we want *these* ones), prepositions ('Keep your hands *away from* the cage'), pronouns ('*She* told *him* not that *she* preferred the Miltonic sonnet, but that *she* liked *it*'), the genitive 'of' ('In several *of* his books, Alexander Solzhenitsyn, a man *of* integrity and a writer *of* the greatest powers, has warned the West *of* the destructive intents *of* Marxism'). These grammatical words and phrases cement together the lexical items (nouns, verbs, adjectives, adverbs). Without these grammatical cementings, we would be reduced to much less sophisticated and often meaningless structures.

Determiners determine number and they particularize; prepositions describe position; conjunctions serve as connectives for clauses and phrases and words and lists (and... and...); the genitive 'of' is used for possession ('the poems of Ratushinskaya'), and also for apposition ('city of London'), character ('woman of integrity'), distribution ('a few of us'), material ('rod of iron'), origin ('a man of Babylon'), quality ('a work of brilliance'), relation ('witnesses of an accident') and subject ('a book of butterflies', 'a book of wisdom').

Language is unable to dispense with these particles and still act with clarity, vigour and good sense. Hebrew, Greek and Latin, sophisticated tongues, have arrays of these particles, and English is rich in them too. We don't want to follow the downward trend of culture into which technology is trying to seduce us.

So, the highly elliptical forms of electronic chit-chat are of no use outside their context: economy and teenage playfulness. It is of use for neither proper conversation nor proper writing. And as most or all of it is juvenile, unattractive and already clichéd, it is of no use for grown-up users of language. At best, we'll reap from it a few witty words which might achieve lexical status: RUOK? WAN2TLK? CUB48, CYA, WUSIWUG (what you see is what you get). No, I don't think so. Such efficient forms of 'nettiquette' and acronyms perhaps serve a use for their own restricted context, but out of that context they are mechanical, robotic, of no humanistic appeal. I have a sample of this new techno-speak, supposed to be so exciting, but it's so embarrassingly unattractive that I can't bring myself to type it out. Telegrams required similar economies, and they made no effect on the structure of language. To regress to electronic forms of language would be a sinking into a barbarism which is beneath the human spirit.

Here is a short passage I have translated from the opening of the Apostle Paul's letter to the Ephesians, reflecting his original syntax (adding in italics, for English sense, a few words omitted in Paul's Greek):

Blessed *be* the God and Father of the Lord of us, Jesus Christ, Who has blessed us in every spiritual blessing *which is* among the most exalted *who are* in Christ, just as He chose us in Him in advance of *the* overthrow of *the* world, for us to be holy and blameless before Him, in love.

Now, without English also having a similarly impressive array of particles as Greek has, it would not be possible to render that passage in such an edifying manner, nor so sober and reverent.

All in all, I sense that arguments against Standard English are not detailed arguments which have anything to do with language, but are to do with politics: down with everything old; make everything new; that's democracy innit. This is revolutionary change from the least competent users and least aesthetically pleasing trends: sometimes change for change's sake, not beneficial change filtering from the top. By 'the top' I mean the best writers and carers of our language.

While it is true that English in its history has undergone several major changes, because of the current politics of dumbing-down this is not a good time intellectually or spiritually for another one of those major changes. The motivations for current attacks, it seems to me, are attacks against something good, rather than an invigorating injection of something which could heighten the quality of English. On the contrary, the arguments only seem to want to downgrade and lower it.

ON THE OTHER HAND....

On the other hand, in our defence of some agreed form of Standard English, we should make four vital comments.

First, although *Grammar Without Groans* speaks in terms of grammatical rights and wrongs, we should not imagine that our language is fixed for today and for all time. If that were so, English might become another dead language, like Latin. Language is never fixed – otherwise we wouldn't have had English in the first place. We'd be speaking the language of Noah. Language changes in its grammar, style, word usage and punctuation. The Early Modern English of Shakespeare and the preface to *The Authorised Bible* have some slight differences in all those features (grammar, style, word usage and punctuation) from those of our day.

When language changes, all it should be doing is disposing of tired forms and adjusting to needs. If it does that well, it is doing a good job, although not all changes are necessarily meritorious. Some are deleterious, some neutral, some useful, some hotly contested.

There's pleasure for most users of language in creating new

words, new sounds and discovering new metaphors, like the joy of hearing the music of the Italian language. So writers, poets, linguists, manufacturers and speakers create novelties. It's part of being human. American jazzmen tired of calling wedding-rings by that name, so they called them 'handcuffs'. There's an initial grin, but by overuse, the delight fades, like yesterday's food. It's as if the paint peels off the old house. The joke is over. So we constantly recreate from other fertile sources of language in order to decorate our speech and writing. Our lexicons receive these new words; then they are dated, then archaic, then discarded. Grammar, though, like punctuation, is slower, much more reluctant to admit novelty, reluctant to budge an inch, and this provides stability in the language and so, ultimately, some degree of stability in ourselves. (Just as it would be true to say that a nation whose language is undergoing vast development or is fading is a nation in a state of instability.)

Second, we should not make the daft mistake of equating language standards with moral standards. A faultless (and sometimes pedantic) user of Standard English is no more nor no less likely to be a moral man, nor even a nice person, than any uneducated speaker. That line of thinking goes back to the Renaissance and even before, linking study and knowledge with morality and religious clericalism. It is probably true, though, that moral declines will accompany degradations of language. I think it's this that puts the finger on the reason why discussions of language are often emotive. If our speech and writing are being criticized, we feel that it's a criticism of our personality. I doubt that language affects morality; I do suspect that morality affects language.

Third, some departures from Standard English are not necessarily bad grammar or wrong, but are a matter of literary style. We should note particularly that creative writing sometimes deliberately departs from Standard English conventions for different effects, particularly in poetry. These departures include disrupted syntax, neologisms (new words, or familiar words or phrases used in a new way), colloquialisms and even eye-dialects (unconventional spelling to imitate regional accents and dialects). Because of their literary context, these deviations would not be spoken of as bad English.

The movement of the Russian Formalists in the 1920s noted deviations from conventional language as the most outstanding characteristic of what defines 'literariness' from non-'literariness'. A long time before the Russian Formalists, though, Aristotle in his *Poetics* wrote of his ideal for the diction of poetry:

> **an impressive diction [is] one that escapes the ordinary, results from the use of strange words, by which I mean foreign words, metaphors, expanded words, and whatever departs from normal usage... The language in which these things are narrated will include foreign words and metaphors and various abnormalities of diction, for this is a licence we grant to the poets.**

But before we can embark effectively on inventing literary deviations and escaping the ordinary, it should go without saying that we must first have a knowledge of the standardized form from which we are departing. As Robert Graves said somewhere, a poet should:

> **master the rules of grammar before he attempts to bend or break them.**

Fourth, if we are going to uphold the most edifying aesthetic values of language, it would be more helpful to speak not so much of a standard (whose?), but of standards defined by aesthetics, clear thinking and sophistication.

So, why do I defend standards in our spoken and written language? First, because care and interest in our language preserves its best elements and allows it to be invigorated with new forms; and second, the skilful use of language is a great pleasure: that's enough.

Chris Sparkes
April 2004

BIBLIOGRAPHY

Kingsley Amis, *The King's English: A Guide to Modern Usage*, Harper Collins (1980)

Bill Bryson, *Mother Tongue*, Penguin (1991)

E.W. Bullinger, *Figures of Speech in the Bible*, Eyre and Spottiswoode, (1898)

Steven Croft & Robert Myers, *Exploring Language & Literature*, Oxford University Press (2000)

David Crystal, *Dictionary of Linguistics and Phonetics*, 4th edition, Blackwell (1980)

David Crystal, *Encyclopaedia of the English Language*, Cambridge University Press (1995)

J.A. Cuddon, *Dictionary of Literary Terms and Literary Theory*, Penguin (1982), 4th edition (1999)

H.W. Fowler & F.G. Fowler, *The King's English*, Oxford University Press (1906), 3rd edition (1936)

Robyn Gee & Carol Watson, *English Grammar*, Usborne (1990)

Ernest Gowers, *The Complete Plain Words*, HMSO (1986)

David Graddol, Jenny Cheshire & Joan Swann, *Describing Language*, 2nd edition, Open University Press (1998)

George Keith & John Shuttleworth, *Living Language*, Hodder & Stoughton (1997)

Martin H. Manser, ed., *Good Word Guide*, Bloomsbury (1990)

George Orwell, *Inside the Whale*, Penguin (1957)

Olivia Smith, *The Politics of Language: 1791-1819*, Oxford University Press (1986)

Sara Thorne, *Mastering Advanced English Language*, Macmillan (1997)

R. Larry Trask, *The Penguin Dictionary of English Grammar*, Penguin (2000)

Lynne Truss, *Eats, Shoots & Leaves: The Zero Tolerance Approach to Punctuation*, Profile Books (2003)

Quick-glance Index